DATE DUE

Educational Research Fifth Edition

A Guide for Preparing a Thesis
or Dissertation Proposal in Education

D1479376

WITHDRAWN

Educational Research Fifth Edition

A Guide for Preparing a Thesis or Dissertation Proposal in Education

Meredith D. Gall
University of Oregon

Walter R. Borg
Utah State University

with contributions by

Gary E. Lietke
Phillip C. Mendel
Sandra M. Simons
Neal B. Strudler

Longman
New York & London

Educational Research: An Introduction, Fifth Edition
A Guide for Preparing a Thesis or Dissertation Proposal in Education

Longman Inc., 95 Church Street, White Plains, N.Y. 10601

Associated companies:
Longman Group Ltd., London
Longman Cheshire Pty., Melbourne
Longman Paul Pty., Auckland
Copp Clark Pitman, Toronto
Pitman Publishing Inc., New York

ISBN: 0-8013-0385-0

89 90 91 92 93 94 9 8 7 6 5 4 3 2 1

CONTENTS

Note to the Instructor

Part I. The "Mini" Dissertation Proposal   1

Introduction   1

Assigning Students to Write a "Mini" Proposal   1

Benefits of the Assignment   3

Handout A.   Student Assignment: Writing a "Mini"
              Dissertation Proposal   5
Handout B.   Dissertation Proposal Outline   8

Part II. Examples of Dissertation Proposals   14

Introduction   14

A. Dissertation Proposal for a Laboratory   17
    Experiment -- Gary E. Lietke
              Introduction   18
              Review of the Literature   26
              Method   46
              Bibliography   54

B. Dissertation Proposal for a Descriptive/   61
    Correlational Study -- Philip C. Mendel
              Introduction   62
              Review of the Literature   70
              Method   71
              Bibliography   76

C. Dissertation Proposal for a Field-based   78
    Quasi-Experiment -- Sandra M. Simons
              Introduction   79
              Review of the Literature   83
              Method   97
              Bibliography   108

D. Dissertation Proposal for a Qualitative
    Research Study -- Neal B. Strudler   113
              Introduction   114
              Method   118
              Appendices   122
              Bibliography   140

NOTE TO THE INSTRUCTOR

We make reference throughout this guide to the dissertation proposal. Most of our comments apply as well to the thesis proposal. The only substantial difference between a proposal for thesis research at the master's level and a proposal for dissertation research at the doctoral level is that the thesis proposal usually is briefer. This is so because master's students typically select simpler research problems and simpler research methodology than do doctoral students.

The guide is not tied specifically to the textbook Educational Research: An Introduction, Fifth Edition, published by Longman. Therefore, use of any part of this guide does not necessitate use of the textbook in a particular way. Preparation of a dissertation proposal, however, requires the student to have knowledge about specific aspects of research methodology. These areas of prerequisite knowledge are noted in the guide, together with the chapters of the textbook where the knowledge is presented.

Meredith D. Gall
Walter R. Borg

PART I

THE "MINI" DISSERTATION PROPOSAL

INTRODUCTION

Preparing a dissertation proposal is one of the most difficult tasks to confront a student in a doctoral program. Many students do not think about the dissertation until they have completed all coursework and have passed their comprehensive examinations. These students usually have a poor understanding of the dissertation process and no clearly defined research interest. Consequently, many of them drop out of the doctoral program at this point. A student in this situation often is referred to as an "A.B.D." (All But Dissertation).

One way to help students avoid becoming A.B.D. is to familiarize them with the dissertation process early in their doctoral program. This can be done by having students prepare a proposal as an assignment in a research methods course taken early in the graduate program. This proposal can be much briefer than a formal dissertation proposal. Also, it need not involve the research problem that the student will pursue for the actual dissertation. For this reason, we call it "mini proposal" or "mock proposal."

ASSIGNING STUDENTS TO WRITE A "MINI" PROPOSAL

The assignment described below was designed for use by instructors of research methods courses. It also can be used by dissertation advisers to help a student get started on the proposal-writing process.

Students find the assignment helpful because it simplifies the process of writing a dissertation proposal. Also, it demystifies the process, thereby reducing the dissertation anxiety that many students experience.

The basic assignment is for students to write a "mini" dissertation proposal. It is a "mini" proposal because it typically is 7-10 pages in length, whereas an actual dissertation proposal might be 25 pages or more.

The assignment is described in Handout A at the end of this part of the guide. You are welcome to use this handout as is or to adapt it for your own purposes.

You will notice that the handout is highly structured, with prespecified headings. This is to help students structure their thinking and focus on the key elements of a dissertation proposal.

In some cases, the research problem chosen for this assignment will turn out to be the student's actual dissertation problem. If so, the "mini" proposal can be revised, without much difficulty, to fit the format required by your department.

We have found it helpful to break the mini-proposal assignment into a set of smaller assignments. Handout B can be used for this purpose. It is presented at the end of this part of the guide.

Handout B is a detailed, fill-in-the-blank outline. It structures the student's thinking even more than the proposal outline contained in Handout A. Despite its high degree of structure, Handout B has sufficient flexibility to accommodate a variety of quantitative and qualitative research designs.

You can ask students to complete part of Handout B every other class session or so and to hand it in as an assignment. You can read the assignment and return it to the students the following class session with feedback and an "OK" or "Needs further work." Students who receive the latter response should redo the assignment.

We have had good success in having students complete Handout B as a set of seven assignments during a course on research methods. Each assignment asks students to complete one of the seven parts of the outline. You can time the assignments to correspond to readings in Educational Research: An Introduction, Fifth Edition and to class sessions in which you discuss particular topics. The seven assignments and corresponding chapters in the textbook are as follows:

1. Purpose of study -- Chapter 2 (Developing the Research Proposal)

2. Research objectives -- Chapter 2

3. Literature search -- Chapter 4 (Reviewing the Research Literature)

4. Variables -- Chapter 2

5.   Measures -- Chapter 7 (<u>Selection and Administration of Tests</u>); Chapter 8 (<u>Types of Standardized Tests</u>); Chapter 11 (<u>The Methods and Tools of Survey Research</u>); Chapter 12 (<u>The Methods and Tools of Observation Research</u>)

6.   Sample -- Chapter 6 (<u>Populations and Samples</u>)

7.   Research Design -- Chapter 9 (<u>Quantitative Research Design and Statistical Analysis</u>); Chapter 10 (<u>Qualitative Research</u>); also, chapters in Part V (Basic Types of Educational Research)

Because the assignments are cumulative, you should consider asking students to hand in their preceding completed assignments, together with the current assignment. In this way, you can remind yourself of the purpose of the proposed study and see how the various parts of the proposal interrelate. Many students use a word processor for their coursework, so it is easy for them to prepare a cumulative proposal outline.

Students need not reproduce Handout B in its entirety and write in the specified spaces. They can simply write each relevant heading of the handout or its indicator (e.g. 6.A), followed by their response to it.

As students complete the parts of Handout B and learn more about educational research, some will want to change their research problems. We allow students in our courses to make the change, but they are asked to redo all of the preceding assignments relating to Handout B, in addition to doing the current assignment.

After students complete the various sections of Handout B, you can give them the final assignment of organizing the information on it into a coherent paper that corresponds to the proposal outline shown in Handout A. This paper constitutes the mini-dissertation proposal.

Benefits of the Assignment

We find that assigning students to write a mini-dissertation proposal in a research methods course has several benefits, especially if the course is offered early in the students' graduate program.

First, the assignment gives students an early opportunity to think about possible dissertation problems. Although we allow students to select any research problem for the assignment, most students identify problems in their areas of interest. In some cases, the problem chosen for the assignment becomes their actual dissertation problem or is closely related to it.

The obvious advantage of thinking about a dissertation problem at the start of a graduate program is that students can develop and refine it as they complete required coursework and prepare for comprehensive examinations. Also, the assignment reduces the threat of the impending dissertation, because students see it for what it really is rather than what they imagine it to be.

Another benefit of the assignment is that it allows students to practice most of the important parts of the research process. They have the opportunity to identify a meaningful research problem; formulate hypotheses, objectives, and variables; review the research literature; select an appropriate research design; consider ethical and human relations issues; select data analysis procedures; and create a time line for completing a study.

The only limitation is that the proposal-writing assignment does not give students practice in collecting, analyzing, and interpreting data. You can assign this type of practice by having students actually conduct their proposed research, at least to the point of doing a pilot study. There probably is not enough time in a one-term research methods course to assign a pilot study, but it might be possible in a two-term course. Another option is to have students use a data bank to practice working with data. The assignment section of the Instructor's Manual for <u>Educational Research: An Introduction, Fifth Edition</u>, describes how this can be done.

The mini-dissertation assignment is a good way to develop student interest in the content of the research methods course. As each aspect of the research process is covered in lectures and the textbook, students can see its direct relevance to the thesis or dissertation that they must do to earn a graduate degree, which is their ultimate goal.

We recommend that you emphasis to students that the mini-dissertation assignment is not just an academic exercise. It represents an important step in actual educational research. Professional researchers go through an initial phase in which they set forth the design of a study in a planning document. If the researcher intends to seek funding for the study, this document will be critical to the success of the effort.

The second author has given the assignments contained in Handouts A and B in his research methods class over the past ten years. Student reaction have been consistently positive. Students appreciate the relevance of the assignments to the dissertation that looms on their horizons. They also appreciate how completing Handout B over a series of seven assignments allows them to break a large, overwhelming task into small, manageable tasks and to receive immediate feedback from the instructor.

Student Assignment:

Writing a "Mini" Dissertation Proposal

The purpose of this assignment is to practice writing a doctoral dissertation proposal. The proposal should be 7-10 pages in length. It should describe each step of the research process. Follow the outline given below using the headings and subheadings that I have provided. (If you think your proposal should follow a different outline, please let me know in advance.) Be sure to respond to each question and specification given in the outline. This assignment is due on the last scheduled meeting of the course--December 8.

Introduction

1. _Purpose of Study_. State the purpose of the study in one or two sentences.

2. _Variables_. Identify all pertinent variables. Define each variable in a sentence or two, and indicate whether you are viewing each variable as independent or dependent in the context of your research design.

3. _Background_. What led you to formulate this particular research problem? What social, educational, political, and/or research factors provide a context for understanding why this study is worth doing?

4. _Significance of Study_. How will your study contribute to knowledge about education?

5. _Research Hypotheses, Objectives, or Questions_. Indicate the specific purposes of the study in the form of hypotheses, objectives, and/or questions. You should formulate a research problem of sufficient scope to require at least three such statements.

Review of Literature

6. <u>Sources</u>. List the key descriptors (at least two) that you used to guide your bibliographic search. List at least two preliminary sources and at least one literature review (or bibliography) that you consulted. Photocopy one page from each of these three sources that shows the pertinent descriptor and references; identify your source on each copies page. Include the copied pages as an appendix to your proposal.

7. <u>Review</u>. Describe at least two major studies or theoretical/opinion papers relevant to your research problem. Discuss how they are relevant. Describe how you would organize your review of the literature (e.g., chronologically, topically).

Method

8. <u>Research Design</u>. Describe your design--descriptive, correlational, experimental, R&D, historical. What are the weaknesses and limitations of the design? Are there threats to internal and external validity in the design?

9. <u>Sample</u>. Describe your sampling procedure. Specify the population that you will study, or from which you will draw a sample, or to which you will generalize.

10. <u>Measures</u>. Re-list all of the variables states above (item 2 above). Indicate how each variable will be measured. If you need to develop measures, how will you establish their validity and reliability? If you select already developed measures, what are their psychometric properties?

Data Analysis

12. <u>Statistics</u>. Re-state each of your hypotheses, objectives, and/or questions (item 5 above). Indicate the measures relevant to each one and the descriptive statistics that will be used to test each hypothesis or to respond to a research objective/question. Also indicate appropriate inferential statistics. Show simulated data if they will help to explain your statistical procedures.

Time Line

    13. <u>Time Line</u>. Make a breakdown of the events (and approximate dates or amounts of time) that need to occur to complete the study.

Dissertation Proposal Outline

1. PURPOSE OF STUDY

    A. (One sentence only.) The purpose of this study
        is _____

        _____

        _____

        _____

    B. What study or literature review is your study based
    on?

       (Give citation) _____

       _____

    C. How does your study build on previous research?
       (No more than three sentences. _____

       _____

       _____

       _____

       _____

       _____

       _____

2. RESEARCH OBJECTIVES

   A. In what form are you stating your research objectives?
   (Check one or more)

   _____ Objectives

   _____ Questions

   _____ Hypotheses

   B. My research questions/hypotheses/objectives are:

   a._____

   _____

   b._____

   _____

   c._____

   _____

   d._____

3. LITERATURE SEARCH

   A. I will use these descriptors in my literature search:

   a. _____

   b. _____

   c. _____

   d. _____

   B. I will consult these bibliographic sources in my literature search:

   a. _____

   b. _____

4. VARIABLES

What are the variables? Also circle whether they are
Independent, Dependent, or Neither.

a. I N D _____

b. I N D _____

c. I N D _____

d. I N D _____

e. I N D _____

f. I N D _____

5. MEASURES

Restate each variable identified in Part 4. For each
variable, indicate how you will measure it
(questionnaire item, test, observational rating, etc.);
the type of scale it is (category, dichotomy,
continuous scale); whether it will be developed or
selected; relevant types of reliability (e.g.,
internal, inter-rater, stability); and relevant types
of validity (e.g., content, construct, predictive). If
you have several variables that will be measured the
same way, list them together.

a. Variable(s) _____

Measure _____

Scale type _____

To be developed _____To be selected_____

Reliability _____

Validity _____

b. Variable(s) _____

Measure _____

Scale type _____

To be developed _____To be selected _____

Reliability _____

Validity _____

c. Variable(s) _____

Measure _____

Scale type _____

To be developed _____ To be selected _____

Reliability _____

Validity _____

6. SAMPLE

A. My sample will consist of (check one)

people _____   things _____ events _____

that have these characteristics:

_____

_____

_____

_____

B. My sampling procedure will be (check one)

random _____

nonrandom _____

C. My sample size will be _____ because

_____

_____

_____

D. My sample will include subgroups (check one).

        Yes _____   No _____

If yes, the subgroups are:

   a. _____
   b. _____
   c. _____
   d. _____

E. The unit of analysis will be (check one).

       Groups _____   Individuals _____

7.   RESEARCH DESIGN

A. My research design is (check one more):

Descriptive _____

Correlational _____

Experimental _____

B. If your design is descriptive, are your variables
(Check one or more):

Prespecified? _____

To be discovered? _____

What statistics will you use to analyze the data?

_____

_____

_____

C. If your design is correlational, what variable(s)
will be correlated with what other variable(s)?

_____

_____

_____

What statistics will you use to analyze the data?

_____

_____

_____

D. If your design is experimental, what is (are) the independent variable(s)?

_____

_____

_____

_____

What is (are) the dependent variable(s)?

_____

_____

_____

What type of experimental design will be employed?

_____

What statistics will you use to analyze the data?

_____

_____

_____

PART II

Examples of Dissertation Proposals

INTRODUCTION

Graduate students appreciate the opportunity to read examples of actual dissertation proposals. The examples are a useful aid in understanding the proposal-writing process described in Chapter 2 of Educational Research: An Introduction, Fifth Edition. Also, they provide a model when it comes time for students to prepare their own proposal. This part of the guide includes four proposals that you can give to students for these purposes.

The proposals are presented nearly in the form that they were submitted to a dissertation committee for approval. The only changes involved minor editing, deletion of several lengthy appendices (they can be found in the completed dissertations), and where necessary, deletion of names of persons, places, and institutions mentioned in the proposal.

The proposals do not correspond exactly to the studies as they were executed. Each of them was approved, but contingent upon making certain revisions in response to the committee's criticisms and recommendations. Further changes were made as each study progressed. In this respect, dissertation proposals are somewhat like blueprints used in building construction. Blueprints often are revised, and missing details filled in, as materials are ordered and construction begins. Dissertation proposals, too, are rarely complete, nor are they cast in concrete. The methodology specified in a proposal is often revised as the student develops new insights and encounters unexpected problems.

You may wish to have your students examine this process of change and revision in a research study. For this reason, we selected proposals that resulted in completed dissertations. Copies of the dissertations are available from University Microfilms International (UMI). For ordering information, call the toll-free number 800-521-3042 or write: UMI Dissertation Information Service, 300 North Zeeb Road, Ann Arbor, Michigan 48106. The ordering number for each dissertation precedes the proposal.

Advisors and departments vary in the amount of detail they require in a dissertation proposal. Also, the nature of the research problem affects the amount of required detail. For these and other reasons, several of the proposals in this guide are more elaborate than others. For example, the proposal by Gary Lietke contains an extensive literature review, whereas the proposal by Neal Strudler highlights only the major reports relating to his dissertation problem. You should consult with your advisor to determine how detailed each section of the proposal should be. The proposals in this guide provide examples of the range of detail that can be included.

The first dissertation proposal, by Gary E. Lietke, involved an experiment with a factorial design. Unlike the other three proposals, the study was conducted in a laboratory-like setting. This type of setting allows for tight research controls. The studies described in the other three proposals were conducted in actual school settings, where research controls are more difficult to achieve. The purpose of the laboratory experiment was to determine the relative effectiveness of different types of questions inserted into video materials, and whether the effectiveness of the questions is affected by learner characteristics. The dissertation proposal was given an award for excellence by the Association for Educational Communications and Technology in 1981. The findings of the completed study were presented at the 1983 annual meeting of the American Educational Research Association.

The second dissertation proposal, by Phillip C. Mendel, was for a study that involved both descriptive and correlational research designs. The purpose of the descriptive part of the study was to identify the level of morale and work-site satisfaction of a specific population of teachers. The correlational part of the study involved a search for factors that affect teachers' morale and work-site satisfaction. A paper based on the completed dissertation was presented to the Fifth Annual Pacific Educational Conference in 1988.

The third dissertation proposal, by Sandra M. Simons, was for a study that involved a quasi-experimental design. (The design was quasi-experimental, because subjects were not randomly assigned to treatments.) The purpose of the study was to develop and test an instructional strategy to improve the ability of secondary school students to comprehend textbook material. The completed study was selected by the International Reading Association as one of the ten best dissertations on reading in 1985. An article reporting part of the study appeared in the February 1989 issue of <u>Journal of Reading</u> (pp. 419-428).

The final dissertation proposal, by Neal B. Strudler, was for a qualitative research study. Its purpose was to examine the roles and characteristics of elementary teachers who were selected to be school-based change agents to bring about implementation of computer education. The study involved a set of case studies using a variety of research methodologies -- questionnaires, interviews, direct observation, and document analysis. A paper reporting the findings of the dissertation was reported at the 1988 annual meeting of the American Educational Research Association. A chapter reporting the study will appear in the forthcoming book <u>Case Studies in Computer-Assisted Learning</u> to be published by Falmer Press.

Gary E. Lietke

Dissertation Proposal

Higher-cognitive and Lower-cognitive Inserted
Postquestions in Video Instruction: Effects of Treatments
and Aptitude-Treatment Interactions on Student
Learning

Information about the completed dissertation is in
Dissertation Abstracts International, vol. 44, no. 11,
section A, page 3252.
The DAI order number is DEQ 84-03743.

INTRODUCTION

Problem to be Addressed

How can film and videotape materials be improved so that they are used more effectively in college level instruction? Which students might benefit (or lose) by modifying the traditional passive experience of learning by film and videotape so that it becomes an experience of participation?

The purpose of this study is to determine whether individual learner characteristics interact with different video/film instructional formats to affect student learning. Specifically, this study will test the effectiveness of video materials with higher-cognitive inserted postquestions, lower-cognitive inserted postquestions, or no inserted questions, and whether their effectiveness is mediated by learner characteristics of general intelligence, content area aptitude, verbal aptitude, film memory aptitude, attitude toward instructional video/film, experience with entertainment video/film, and experience with instructional video/film.

Background of Problem

Videotape and film, while their content, technical production, and distribution processes appear to be reasonably sound, are not being used in college instruction to the degree forecast by past media proponent visionaries. In contrast, as a result of the post World War II technology movement, community college, military, and industrial training settings have made considerable use of these media.

The difference in instructional focus between those who heavily utilize these media (community colleges, military, industry) and those who lightly use them (liberal arts and four-year colleges and universities) may point to one quite important reason why film and videotape are not being used more than they are in college instruction. Traditionally this difference in focus has been contrasted as "training" versus "educating," terms which also generally distinguish between "recall" and higher-order "thinking" outcomes (Bloom, 1956). Thus the question arises: is film/videotape capable of facilitating the higher-order, thinking outcomes philosophically espoused and emphasized by college and university faculties?

Instructional research has as one of its goals the improvement of instructional methods. One instructional

- 18 -

researcher, Rothkopf (1970), is credited for originating the concept of "mathemagenic" activities. Mathemagenic activities are instructional activities designed to assist the student in learning more from a given information presentation than he might have learned without such a mathemagenic aid. The most commonly used mathemagenic aids are advance organizers, statement of instructional objectives, and inserted questions.

A great deal of research has evaluated the validity of these various mathemagenic activities over the years, particularly when applied to the print medium, or prose. Some of the most promising results have involved the use of inserted questions -- also known as adjunct questions. Inserted questions are testlike questions which relate to the specific content of the information presentation. There are various types of these questions: (1) prequestions, (2) postquestions, (3) inserted prequestions, and (4) inserted postquestions. Prequestions prepare the student for the content that will be covered in the information presentation. Postquestions follow the presentation and challenge the student to review, either directly or mentally by memory, the content for their answers. Inserted prequestions and postquestions are interspersed periodically throughout the presentation, serving either of the above two functions, that is, preparation or review.

Most of the early mathemagenic research examined for treatment main effects and was directed to questions and measures at the recall (lower-order) level. (Main effects are produced when the average performance of a given treatment group is significantly different from the average performance of at least one other treatment group.) Although the results were not always positive, main effects in support of inserted questions, especially inserted postquestions, were the trend. Inserted recall-level questions generally increase student learning achievement when measured by recall test measures.

But in this past decade an additional purpose has been intended for inserted questions. In addition to recall outcomes, educators have become increasingly interested in higher-order cognitive instructional outcomes. Mathemagenic researchers likewise have attempted to determine whether learning as measured by higher-order test criteria could be facilitated by inserted questions.

Current inserted question research examines both lower-order and higher-order outcomes in the context of two types of learning: intentional and incidental. Intentional learning is defined as the ability of subjects to produce answers to posttest questions that are identical to inserted questions (both lower-order and higher-order); incidental learning is defined as the ability of subjects to answer posttest questions that are different from the inserted questions, but that cover content in the information presentation. Thus, four types of learning scales can be produced: (1) lower-order intentional, (2) higher-order intentional, (3) lower-order incidental, and (4) higher-order incidental. Again, most of these inserted-questions studies have examined prose. results of these studies investigating both recall and higher-order inserted questions and outcomes are less conclusive than the previously discussed results of studies on lower-order (only) inserted questions and measures. However, the trends favor (1) inserted postquestions as the most effective adjunct question type and (2) higher-order (or possibly a mix of higher- and lower-order) inserted questions as facilitators of higher-order (and lower-order, as well) outcomes, especially for incidental learning.

A good example of this current approach to inserted question research is a study of 87 junior college students by Shavelson, Berliner, Ravitch, and Loeding (1974a). They compared treatments of higher-order inserted prequestions, higher-order inserted postquestions, lower-order inserted prequestions, and lower-order inserted postquestions and a control group of no inserted questions for their effects on achievement. Immediate and delayed measures for both higher- and lower-order levels and for both intentional and incidental learning were administered. In general, the higher-order inserted postquestion treatment facilitated the most learning, significantly more than the lower-order inserted prequestions. For intentional learning, the control group performed worse than all treatment groups; but for incidental learning the control group and the higher-order inserted postquestion group, with almost equal group means, outperformed the other three groups.

Because the Shavelson et al. study addresses the significant aspects of the proposed dissertation study (namely, inserted question level, measures of higher- and lower-order learning, intentional and incidental learning, college student population), this study has been chosen as the main basis for designing the proposed study.

While mathemagenic research on prose has been constant and prolific, such cannot be said about mathemagenic research relating to nonprint media, including film and videotape. The differences between prose and fixed-sequence, fixed-pace media such as videotape, film, and slide-tape are significant. Readers of prose determine their own pace, can pause to reflect or reread a portion of text during its initial reading, and can search and review the text even after its initial reading. Viewers of videotape and film must usually observe and process the information at the pace determined by its producers. They cannot pause to reflect or review during viewing; and they can rarely search and review the presentation after viewing it. These differences between prose and video media suggest that inserted questions may have different effects in the two types of media.

The promise of inserted question methodology is to transform fixed-sequence, fixed-pace media from a quite passive learning activity into a more participatory learning activity. Thus some research has examined mathemagenic activities in fixed-sequence, fixed-pace media.

Early film research of the 1950s and early 60s did include some studies of inserted questions in film (e.g., Michael and Maccoby, 1953; May, Lumsdaine, and Hadsell, 1958). Like the early prose studies, learning by film was found to be facilitated by inserted questions, especially postquestions. The inserted questions and outcome measures were at the lower cognitive levels. These results were consistent, but the number of studies was relatively small.

Since this early era of film research, only three studies have been reported which investigate the effects of inserted questions in fixed-sequence, fixed-pace media: two studies of slide-tape presentations (Dayton, 1977; Dayton and Schwier, 1979), and one study of videotape (Heestand, 1979). Despite the current paradigm favoring higher-level learning, the Dayton and Dayton and Schwier investigations addressed neither higher-level learning activities nor higher-level outcomes. The Heestand dissertation is not yet available for examination [at the time that this proposal was written].

Another important development in instructional research of the past decade is the study of "aptitude-treatment interaction", or "ATI." Its proponents (e.g., Cronbach and Snow, 1977) believe that some instructional treatments may not equally facilitate learning in all students, but rather that certain treatments might benefit certain students who have certain characteristics and other treatments might benefit other students who have another set of characteristics. This research paradigm has gained a full head of steam and is now being applied to mathemagenic research and media research as well.

ATI research in the areas of inserted questions and videotape/film media suggests a number of aptitudes that might interact with these two instructional techniques. Again, the Shavelson et al. (1974a) study is of special relevance to the proposed study. These researchers also examined for ATIs, and found verbal aptitudes to interact significantly with inserted question treatments. Learners high in verbal aptitude measures did not benefit from the higher-order inserted postquestion treatment as much as low aptitude learners. Lower-order inserted prequestions seemed to benefit low and high aptitude learners approximately equally. High aptitude learners learned more than low aptitude learners under conditions of lower-order postquestions, higher-order inserted prequestions, and no questions. The effects were significant only for the higher-order postquestions, control, and lower-order postquestion treatments. These three treatments will also be the treatments investigated in the proposed study.

It can also be argued that a relationship may exist between general ability and content area ability. It may be that content area ability may interact more strongly with the various instructional treatments than the more indefinite scale of general ability.

Film memory aptitude, attitude toward instructional film, experience with entertainment film, and experience with instructional film are all indirect measures relating to a construct called film literacy. These measures have been demonstrated to interact with film media to affect learning outcomes. Learners who score high on these film literacy aptitude measures learn more from film treatments than those who score low on them. Since the relationship of film literacy to learning from video/film media may be similar to the relationship of verbal aptitude to learning from prose, the same pattern of ATIs found for verbal aptitude and inserted questions in prose may be manifest for film literacy measures and inserted questions in videotape.

In summary, research findings for inserted questions activities and film/video media suggest the desirability of investigating the learner, treatment, and learning outcome variables shown in Table 1.

Table 1. Variables to be Investigated

Learner Aptitudes	Treatments	Learning Outcomes
General intelligence	Videotape only	Higher-order intentional
Content area ability	Videotape with higher-order inserted postquestions	Lower-order intentional
Verbal ability		
Film memory ability	Videotape with lower-order inserted postquestions	Higher-order incidental
Attitude toward TV/film instruction		Lower-order incidental
Experience with TV/film entertainment		

Research Questions

1. (Treatment main effects) Is there a significant difference in performance on the measures of higher-order and lower-order intentional, and higher-order and lower-order incidental learning between groups of students assigned to the three treatments: videotape only (V), videotape with higher-order inserted postquestions (VH), and videotape with lower-order inserted postquestions (VL)?

2. (Learner main effects) Is there a significant difference in performance on the various learning measures between students who score high on measures of: general intelligence, content area ability, verbal ability, film memory ability, attitude toward instructional TV/film, experience with TV/film instruction, and experience with TV/film entertainment, and students who score low on those measures?

3. (Interaction effects) Do learner characteristics interact with treatments to affect performance on learning measures? That is, is a particular treatment equally

effective or ineffective for all students, or is its
effectiveness different for students who score high or low
on a particular aptitude measure?

Significance of the Study

If the hypotheses of this study are supported, the
findings have four potential benefits for education.
First, effectiveness of teaching in the traditional
classroom, especially in four-year colleges and
universities, may be improved by videotapes/films which are
modified by inserted questions to increase learning
outcomes (especially higher-order learning).
Second, budget pressures by higher education
administrators and the contributing and taxpaying public
demand that we improve education by increasing the
efficiency and effectiveness of existing resources, rather
than by developing expensive new alternatives to improve
education. The existing collections of film and videotapes
available and appropriate for college/university
instruction are bountiful if they can be demonstrated to be
effective for instruction. Inexpensive modification of
these materials to include inserted questions may provide
some answer to the demand for cost-effective improvements
in higher education.
Third, an important new application of television/film
is underundergoing rapid development at this time. This
approach is called by a variety of names, for example, the
open university, university outreach programs, and "Campus
of the Air". In this approach, a college or university
brings its services to students who lack physical access to
its usual geographic service environment, rather than
demanding that those students physically attend the
university. Broadcast television is a natural, economical
medium of instruction for achieving this purpose.
Nevertheless many skeptics doubt the effectiveness of
learning by a passive viewing experience. Inserted
questions requiring student viewer participation may
significantly increase the effectiveness of this new higher
education strategy.
Finally, the aptitude-treatment interaction
investigation in this study may improve educational
effectiveness by increasing the potential of matching
students by their aptitudes to instructional strategies.
As this line of research progresses, it may become possible
to counsel a student as to which instructional strategies
are likely to be most effective for his or her learning,
and which courses or other instructional experiences
include those strategies. Likewise an institution might
assess the major types of students it serves and attempt to
offer the instructional strategies which have been

demonstrated to match their aptitude patterns. Obviously this last application is idealistic, but its potential is worthwhile enough that the investigation of ATI effects in this study is desirable.

REVIEW OF THE LITERATURE

Introduction

The purpose of this dissertation is to investigate the
relationship, if any, between learner aptitudes, types of
inserted postquestion treatments, and types of learning
outcomes when the medium of presentation is television. No
public record of research on the specific combination of
variables in this study exists. In fact, very little
research has been conducted on the effects of inserted
questions in film or video. Nevertheless two substantial
bodies of literature generally relate to this research
project: research on inserted questions in written (and
also oral recitation) media, and research on aptitudes
related to learning from TV/film.

This review will survey those bodies of literature in
respect to the present study's (1) dependent variables
(learning outcomes), (2) manipulated independent variables
(inserted postquestion treatments), and (3) non-manipulated
independent variables (aptitudes).

Learning Outcomes

Most of the research on inserted questions has used (1)
intentional and (2) incidental learning as the outcome
measures.

Intentional learning is the extent to which a learner
is able to learn those facts, concepts, processes, etc.
which are directly emphasized for the learner by the
teacher or other instructional medium. In inserted
question research, intentional learning is defined to be
how well the learner is able to answer questions on a
posttest that are identical to the adjunct questions asked
in the presentation.

Incidental learning is the ability to learn those
facts, concepts, processes, etc. which are not directly
emphasized in the instruction. For inserted questions,
incidental learning is measured by the learner's
performance on questions whose answers are found in the
instructional presentation, but the content supplying those
answers is different from that providing the answers to the
intentional learning questions (Richards, 1979; Dayton and
Schwier, 1979).

The other distinction involving learning in the
proposed study is that of higher-order versus lower-order

learning. This distinction reflects differences between two major instructional approaches. A teaching approach prominent in the late nineteenth century was the traditional recitation, whereby a student would be requested to answer questions whose answers were facts and details from presentation of information he was to have studied (Tyack, 1974). That philosophy can be compared with the early twentieth century problem-solving approach to instruction advocated by John Dewey (1912). At issue is whether the goal of learning should be the recall of facts and ideas (lower-order learning) or the processing and manipulation of those facts and ideas (higher-order learning).

A number of classification systems have been developed to define such learning or thinking process differences. The most commonly used system in inserted question research is the one developed by Bloom et al. (1956). Bloom and his colleagues concluded that cognitive processes formed a hierarchy. The most basic process is (1) knowledge, i.e., the recall of information presented by a source outside the learner. Knowledge is labeled a lower-order cognitive process. (2) Comprehension is the next higher step in the taxonomy. The processes of (3) application, (4) analysis, (5) synthesis, and (6) evaluation complete the ladder. Categories (2) through (6) are labeled by Bloom as higher-order cognitive processes. This study, however, will use only categories (3) through (6) to represent higher-order processes, so as to provide a clear distinction between lower-order and higher-order treatments and outcomes.

Today it is commonly accepted that most important educational goals do not entail verbatim recall (Watts and Anderson, 1971). Good learning requires skill in processing information at all the cognitive levels. It also is generally accepted that instruction should be directed toward both intentional and incidental learning outcomes. When one combines these two sets of learning orientations in a 2 x 2 matrix, four categories result: lower-order intentional, higher-order intentional, lower-order incidental, and higher-order incidental. The present study will investigate techniques to promote each of these outcomes.

Another distinction involving learning outcomes is short-term versus long-term learning (Andre, 1979). It is useful to know the short-term effects of instruction for various purposes, for example, to determine whether reteaching or redesign of instruction is necessary. Long-term effects are also important, because theultimate goal of instruction is long-term learning, whereby what is learned in instruction will be available to the learner at any future time. The measurement of duration of learning effects is accomplished by achievement tests administered at different lengths of time from the learning experience, ranging from immediately after the experience (immediate posttests) to various intervals afterwards (delayed posttests).

Testing for various learning outcomes at different intervals will provide data as to whcih variables affect the learner's immediate acquisition and longer-term maintenance of instructional outcomes. The study by Shavelson and colleagues (1974a) investigated learning immediately after the information presentation and after a delay of two weeks. The present study will emply a similar set of measurements.

Treatments

The treatments in this study consist of two components: (1) the videotape medium as a constant and (2) inserted postquestions as a manipulated variable. the question of concern in this section of the literature review, then, is, how do inserted postquestions in videotape affect learning?

History of Inserted Questions Research. Inserted question investigation is a subset of research on "mathemagenic" activities, a concept whose primary development is credited to Rothkopf (1963). Interested first in the written medium, he suggested that a teacher might provide additional activities to the traditional prose text that would induce the reader to more actively particpate in the reading-learning process. Early research in this general area--treating such specific mathemagenic aids as advance organizers, statements of instructional objectives, instructions to take notes or to underline key ideas, and inserted questions--generally found that subsequent recall (lower-level learning), both short- and long-term, increased with the added depth of processing elicited by these mathemagenic activities (Rothkopf, 1976).

Inserted questions developed out of a long tradition of using questioning techniques as an instructional strategy. Plato used questioning dialogue; early lectures on teaching methods discussed questions (Fitch, 1879); early twentieth century texts on teaching methods treated questioning techniques (Holley, 1923); and the recent skills approach to teacher training emphasizes skill in questioning strategies (Joyce and Weil, 1972).

Questions traditionally have been used in recitation and testing activities which follow lectures and reading activities. Questions also have a major role in discussion, which, again, usually follows a lecture, reading, or other information presentation activity. The next logical step was to include the questions in the information presentation itself, rather than as a follow-up activity. Rothkopf (1963) used the label "adjunct questions" to refer to such questions.

Like the general area of mathemagenic activities, most inserted question research has concerned learning from prose (beginning with Germane, 1920; Distad, 1927; Washbourne, 1929; and Holmes, 1931), although some studies have applied the concept to discussion and lectures. Only a very few studies have related inserted questions to video/film media. An occasional reference is made in this review to inserted question research in oral recitation methods. However, because these oral recitation questions tend to be grouped either totally before or after the information presentation, their relationship to the present study of inserted questions is generally not relevant.

For the proposed study, the most critical variables in the questioning treatments are the cognitive level of the inserted questions and the presence or absence of inserted questions. The earliest research on inserted questions looked at lower-order inserted questions relative to no inserted questions as measured by lower-order outcomes. As higher-order learning became an important educational outcome, researchers examined the relative effectiveness of higher-order inserted questions versus lower-order inserted questions versus no questions. Within this phase of research, there were two subphases, the earlier measuring learning only by lower-order outcomes, and the latter employing indexes of both higher- and lower-order learning (Andre, 1979). This section of the literature review, then, will briefly examine the first two of these research stages, and discuss the last, current, stage in more depth. Since most research on inserted questions has examined their effects on learning form prose, that type of research will be reported first in the discussion of each stage, followed by any relevant findings from similar research on other media, especially TV/film.

Lower-order Inserted Questions versus No Inserted Questions. These studies generally showed that student learn more from prose when they are required to answer questions which are inserted into the text (Frase, 1967; Rothkopf and Bisbicos, 1967; Rothkopf, 1966).

Given that inserted questions have a facilitating effect, another issue, that of question position, arises: should the inserted question appear before the portion of text it relates to, or after that portion? With respect to lower-order outcomes from lower-order inserted questions, inserted postquestions have been found to be superior to inserted prequestions (Frase, Patrick, and Schumer, 1970; Frase, 1968b; Rothkopf and Bisbicos, 1967; Rothkopf, 1966). While inserted prequestions clearly facilitate lower-order learning (Rickards, 1979), sometimes even more than inserted postquestions do, the evidence suggests that inserted postquestions are hotter in promoting both intentional and incidental learning (Boker, 1974; McGaw and Grotelueschen, 1972; Rothkopf, 1966; Rothkopf and Bloom, 1970).

One of the most critical characteristics of fixed-sequence, fixed-pace information presentation modes (including video/film) is that they typically require only passive viewing by the learner. Dayton and Schwier (1979) hypothesized that it is reasonable to expect that such media presentations would be more effective if they incorporated features that require the learner to respond actively to the material. Inserting questions within instruction offers one method to promote active learner engagement.

It appears that all of the few studies of inserted questions in fixed-sequence, fixed-pace media have investigated lower-order questions and lower-order outcomes. In their review of the literature, Michael and Maccoby (1953, p.411) stated, "Previous research has demonstrated that learning form a factual film increases with the use of audience participation procedures." Their film study demonstrated that an inserted question treatment produced more intentional learning than either a "just think" treatment or a control treatment (no inserted questions).

The performance of groups of tenth and eleventh graders receiving no questions, inserted prequestions, inserted postquestions, and both inserted pre- and postquestion treatments was compared by May, Lumsdaine, and Hadsell (1958). The ordinal ranking for the treatment groups (best-to-worst) on intentional learning was: combination pre- and postquestion treatment, postquestion treatment, prequestion treatment, and control condition. The authors were concerned initially that inserted questions might weaken incidental learning, but there was no significant difference among groups on this outcome.

In contract, Kantor (1960) found that all treatments--inserted prequestions in film, inserted postquestions in film and no questions--taught his seventh grade subjects equally well.

A film study somewhat related to the present investigation was conducted by Teather and Marchant (1974). All film treatments verbally restated important information during film intervals. One treatment added inserted prequestions; another added inserted postquestions. The verbal-restatement-only treatment increased lower-order intentional learning, but not incidental learning. The performance of the two inserted-question groups was not significantly different from the verbal-restatement-only group.

The most recent experimentation on inserted questions

in fixed-sequence, fixed-pace media is that of Dayton and Schwier (1979), who used slide-tape presentations rather than film or videotape. In one experiment with college freshmen, they found significant main effects for intentional learning; the inserted question treatment group outperformed the treatment group whose questions were presented all together at the end of the presentation. The incidental learning effect was not significant, but the mean of the inserted questions group exceeded that of the grouped questions group which exceeded that of the control group.

In an attempt to replicate the Dayton and Schwier study with juniors in high school, Schwier (1979) again investigated main effects. The intentional learning effect was significant (inserted questions were best), and the incidental learning effect was not significant (inserted questions were a little better than other treatments).

While not unanimous, then, the overall results of the fixed-sequence, fixed-pace media studies employing lower-order inserted questions are consistent with those of prose. Inserted postquestions generally are more effective than inserted prequestions or not questions in promoting incidental learning, and they are more effective than no questions in facilitating intentional learning.

Higher-Order Inserted Questions versus Lower-Order and No Question Treatments. The earliest studies that measured learning effects of inserted questions beyond simple verbatim recall still used questioning treatments and measures of subcategories within the knowledge level of Bloom's taxonomy. Rothkopf and Bisbicos (1967) varied the nature of content material required to answer the inserted questions. Comparing five treatments (questions for proper names, questions for numbers, questions for words or technical terms, questions of the combined categories above, and no questions) they found that the proper names treatment facilitated performance only on the posttest questions for proper names. In contrast, the numbers treatment and technical terms treatment facilitated performance on posttest questions of all three categories (names, numbers, technical terms). While this study was confined to subcategories of knowledge-level outcomes, it does represent the beginnings of research to compare the effects of inserted questions on learning outcomes at different cognitive levels.

Frase (1968a) compared the effects of "broader" inserted questions (e.g., How old were the men in the story?) and "specific" inserted questions (e.g., How old was John?) on recall-level learning outcomes. Interestingly, he found that broader questions led to poorer posttest performance. His explanation was that broad questions may have altered the subjects' conception

of the task so that they did not attend to the specific
material that was included in the posttest.

On the other hand, Watts (1973) found that students who
answered broad inserted questions (e.g., Which man is too
old for his job?) did better on a factual posttest than
students who answered specific inserted questions (e.g.,
How old was John?). Watts suggested that because the
broader questions required inferences and comparisons, the
learner gained more.

Richards and DiVesta (1974) compared the effects of
rote-fact inserted questions (recall of specific details in
topic sentences), meaningful inserted questions (requiring
readers to relate specific details to the general ideas
which were both contained in the text), and no inserted
questions. They found that rote-fact questions facilitated
intentional learning   better than did no questions.
Meaningful questions produced more intentional and
incidental learning than did the other treatment
conditions.

Anderson and Biddle (1975) attempted to show that
paraphrased questions (factual questions whose wording
paraphrases the context around the fact in the reading)
would promote more learning from a prose passage than
verbatim questions (factual questions whose wording is
essentially the same as the context around the fact in the
reading). Over a series of four experiments, they were
unable to show any convincing superiority of paraphrased
questions on posttests consisting of the same questions as
those in the treatments.

In contrast, Andre and Sola (1976) were able to
demonstrate that inserted paraphrased questions led to
greater learning than verbatim questions. The posttest in
this study consisted of questions different from those in
the treatments. The Anderson and Biddle study tested only
direct memory of answers to the inserted questions, whereas
the Andre and Sola posttest teased out the distinction
between direct memory of unassociated facts and the added
dimension of semantic encoding required by the paraphrased
questions. This latter study's results were replicated by
Andre and Womack (1978) and Andre (1978).

In a study employing a higher-order treatment, but
still measuring only lower-order outcomes, Allen (1970)
measured the effects of memory level and higher
prequestions on lower-order learning. In a posttest of
factual questions which dealt with the material covered by
the two questioning treatments, the subjects did better on
posttest questions which related to the information that
had been emphasized by their particular treatment. No
overall difference in facilitation of lower-level learning
was found between treatments.

In a summary of factual posttest studies, Andre (1979)
concluded that inserted questions serve to focus subjects'

attention on <u>particular</u> material. No studies of this type
demonstrated that higher-order questions direct attention
of the learners to additional information, a leading
hypothesis of the early higher-order inserted question
studies.

The last category of inserted question research to be
considered is that comparing higher-order, lower-order, and
no inserted question treatments on measures of both higher-
and lower-order outcomes. Only by including measures of
higher-order outcomes is it possible to determine the full
potential of higher-order questions.

One study of questions in oral recitation is of
interest at this point. In a series of two experiments,
Gall and his colleagues (1978) compared treatments which
differed in proportion of higher-order and lower-order
questions. In experiment two, results indicated that
variation in percentage of higher-order questions does
affect learning. Relative to the 25% and 75% higher-order
question treatments, the 50% higher-order questions
treatment was least effective in promoting knowledge level
acquisition and retention, but showed a slight trend toward
being most effective in promoting higher-order thinking
performance. Generally, the 25% higher-order question
group outperformed the 75% group both on knowledge
acquisition and higher-order cognitive measures, although
differences were small. Overall, the findings were
somewhat inconsistent, and thus the authors called for
further research to determine the effect of more extreme
variations in use of higher-order questions (e.g.,
recitations with all lower-order questions compared to a
treatment of 100% higher-order questions). This last type
of design has been characteristic of inserted questions in
prose research and is the treatment comparison for the
proposed study.

The most important and relevant investigation to the
present study is that by Shavelson, Berliner, Ravitch, and
Loeding (1974a). Their study provides the basis for the
proposed study's research questions and design. Two
treatment variables provided the main comparisons:
cognitive level of question and question position. In
combination, these two variables produced four treatments:
(1) higher-order inserted prequestions, (2) higher-order
inserted postquestions, (3) lower-order inserted
prequestions, and (4) lower-order inserted postquestions.
The fifth treatment was a control condition involving no
inserted questions. A total of 87 junior college subjects
were assigned to the five treatment groups, with treatment
group sizes ranging from 13 to 21. Learning outcomes were
measured on both immediate and delayed (two weeks)
posttests consisting of five scales: intentional learning,
incidental learning, higher- and lower-order transfer, and
total learning (total score for the four other specialized

scales. The concept of transfer in this study was not consonant with the common definition of lateral transfer (Gagne, 1970); rather the two transfer scales in this study were only the two components which together constituted the incidental learning scale.

It should be noted that a conceptual problem exists for these scales. Intentional learning was measured as the treatment group's performance on posttest questions identical to its inserted questions. No provision was made to insure for equivalency (in whatever way that could be argued or measured) between the sets of higher-order and lower-order questions. It is not appropriate to compare the intentional score earned by a lower-order question group and the score earned by a higher-order group when the set of items used to measure the intentional learning for the respective groups is not the same set of items, or even two sets which have equal difficulty and discrimination indexes. Conceptually this kind of comparison is like comparing apples and oranges; the processes of higher-order and lower-order learning are quite different. In addition, because the control group had no inserted questions, it was assigned an artificial score for intentional learning based on the group's combined average scores on what were the inserted questions for the other treatments. Thus the comparison of intentional learning scores for the five treatments is conceptually invalid. Somewhat similar validity questions of equivalency within the scales plague the incidental and transfer scales as well. The total learning index is almost a meaningless construct, composed arbitrarily of all the questions used to determine the various other four learning scales. No explanation was provided for what "total" learning is; it is an operational definition without a defined relationship to reality.

Nevertheless, given the scales as designed, some finding are of interest. The only statistically significant main effect was on the total score measure, where a significant simple effect between higher-order postquestions and lower-order prequestions was found. It should be noted that the power of the study must be estimated to be low due to the small sample size in each treatment group of a design of this type.

The rank order of the treatments on six of the dependent measures is given below. A rank of 1 was given for the highest mean score, and 5 for the lowest.

		Treatments			
Measures	lower preQ	higher preQ	lower postQ	higher postQ	control
Total-immed.	5	2	3.5	1	3.5
-delay	5	2	4	1	3
Intent-immed.	5	1	3	4	5
-delay	4	2	3	1	5
Incid.-immed.	5	3	4	2	1
-delay	4	3	5	1	2

Of interest is the fairly strong showing by higher-order postquestions, the high rank of the control treatment on incidental learning, and the relatively low ranks of the lower-order question treatment. The authors comment that the relative "effectiveness of the higher-order inserted postquestion may lie in its ability to promote review in subjects who ordinarily do not engage in such activities" (p.47).

An attempt to partially replicate the above study was made by Shavelson et al. (1974b). By testing a larger sample, 231 college students, and by using a longer treatment duration (six weeks), they hoped to increase their chances of finding significant differences between treatments. Subjects were assigned to one of four treatment groups: lower-order inserted postquestions; higher-order inserted postquestions; higher-order questions in the first third of the course textbook, prompts for self-questioning in the second third, and text-only in the last third; and text-only as a control. On immediate posttests, the control group outperformed all other groups on all the achievement tests (total, part of textbook, and question type scales) except one. This study may have been subject to procedural problems (e.g., it is not clear how it was insured that students assigned to a treatment followed its directions and actually participated in it). Also, while it is called a replication of the Shavelson et al. (1974a) study, its comparability to the proposed study is limited.

The two studies described above did not differentiate among or label specific cognitive processes involved in the higher-order question treatments and test measures. Other studies have examined the effects of specific types of higher-order cognitive questions. For example, McKenzie (1972) compared comprehension-level inserted questions with knowledge-level inserted questions. Neither type of question influenced recall, but the comprehension questions did facilitate better performance on measures of incidental learning.

Comparing the same levels of questions, Dapra and Felker (1974) found that readers given comprehension-level inserted questions scored higher than readers given knowledge-level inserted questions and control-group readers on a problem-solving posttest, but they did not score higher on a comprehension multiple-choice posttest (both posttests measured incidental learning).

Three studies found main effects for application-level questions. Watts and Anderson (1971) made a comparison of: questions requiring name recall; questions requiring recognition of an example stated in the material as the instance of a concept explained in the material (repeated example questions); and questions requiring application by recognizing new, unfamiliar examples of a concept explained in the material. The application-question treatment group performed much better on new application posttest questions and about as well on name and repeated-example posttest questions as did the name and repeated-example treatment groups. Similar results were obtained by Woods and Andre (1978).

Moore (1975) did not find significant differences on posttests among verbatim, paraphrased (treatment types defined by Anderson and Biddle, 1975), and application-question treatments. But Andre (1979) comments that this study was general; no posttest questions were directly or indirectly related to the inserted questions, and no posttest questions asked for application of concepts involved in the inserted questions.

However, further results conflicting with the findings of Watts and Anderson (1971) came from a study by Andre (1976). A series of three experiments gave inconsistent results when comparing four treatment groups: application pre and post inserted questions and factual pre and post inserted questions. In experiment one, college students given factual prequestions did the best of the treatment groups on new application questions. In experiment two, which also involved college students, no significant differences were found. And in experiment three, high school students given factual pre- or postquestions did significantly better on new application items than did students with application questions.

In a study of evaluation-level versus knowledge-level inserted questions, Hunkins (1969) reported that sixth-grade students who received evaluation level questions scored higher on new evaluation posttest questions than did the knowledge treatment students. This study, however, was flawed by

low interrater reliability for assigning inserted
questions to taxonomy levels and inappropriate statistics
(Andre, 1979).

Several conclusions can be drawn over the
research on higher-order versus lower-order prequestions
and postquestions, as well as controls conditions
involving no questions. Typically, prequestion groups
retain roughly the same amount of material directly
questioned as the postquestion group, and both
lower-order and higher-order question groups retain more
of the questioned material than a reading-only group
(intentional learning). However, postquestion groups
recall more material not actually questioned than a
prequestion group or a reading-only condition.

Possibly because they direct attention to
more information, higher-order questions have usually
facilitated factual posttest performance better than that
of control treatments. And when

> students are given adjunct application
> questions about concepts, as compared to
> adjunct factual questions, their ability
> to use knowledge of the concepts to
> recognize new examples or solve problems
> involving the concepts and principles is
> enhanced. The effects of the questions
> appear to be specific to the concepts
> asked about in the adjunct questions;
> acquisition of other concepts and
> principles discussed is not facilitated
> (Andre, 1979).

Methodological Considerations

The inserted question literature raises some
methodological choices that needed to be made in designing
the proposed study. Most notable are decisions about how
to present the inserted questions in film/video, what type
of responses to request for inserted questions, whether
(and how) to provide feedback to the learner on correct
responses to the inserted questions, whether (and how) to
provide feedback to the learner on correct responses to the
inserted questions, and whether to use a pretest.

Inserted questions can be presented by stopping the
film and orally administering the questions (Michael and
Maccoby, 1953). In the study by May, Lumsdaine, and
Hadsell (1958), prequestions were spliced into the film,
with a voiceover narrator reading the "titles"
(alphanumeric printed questions) appearing visually.
Postquestions were administered on a separate worksheet.

No reason was given by the authors for this difference in
format for the two treatments. Conditions were carefully
controlled by Kantor (1960) so that the inserted questions
which were spliced into the film would appear to be part of
the original production. This was attempted by
photographing the questions at the same level of quality as
the main body of film. The narration for the entire film
was rerecorded along with the questions so that the same
voice would narrate both. Teacher and Marchant (1974)
presented the questions in separate learning booklets.

Because the proposed study is intended to be applicable
to instruction via broadcast television as well as for
classroom use, it will utilize the approach used by May,
Lumsdaine, and Hadsell for their prequestions. All
questions will be visually presented in alphanumeric format
by a character generator, and a voiceover will
simultaneously read the question. A character generator is
a device like a typewriter that produces alphanumeric
characters in television signal.

The two issues for inserted question responses are
whether they should be overt or covert and whether they
should be forced-choice or open-ended, constructed
responses. It is often unclear from the research reports
whether the subjects were either requested to "just think"
about a response to the questions (e.g., Vuke, (1962);
advised to produce a written response; or required to write
a response. It can be argued that when a written response
is not required, the subjects may not fully and
consistently be fulfilling the treatment conditions, thus
impairing the potential effectiveness of the treatment.
And if the treatment conditions are not fully implemented,
true differences between treatments may be obscured.

The research evidence is insufficient to determine
whether inserted questions should be presented in a
forced-choice mode (e.g., true-false or multiple-choice) or
open-ended, constructed response mode. In a rare study
comparing the two options, Frase (1968b) found no
significant differences between these two response modes
for lower-order learning. The study by Shavelson, et al.
(1974a), on which the proposed study is based, employed
multiple-choice responses. However, one of the authors,
Berliner (Note 1), now advocates that open-ended,
short-answer responses are the most appropriate for adjunct
question research. It is possible that even for
lower-order questions, forced-choice answers provide cueing
effects that impair the facilitating effect of the question
by reducing the depth of processing necessary to answer the
question. For higher-order questions, the problem of
forced-choice response is even more serious because
higher-order cognitive processes require, by definition,
open-ended thinking that is unique to the thinker's own
experiences, ideas, and expression. Additionally, for

higher-order questions many responses can accurately answer
the question. For example, it is clear from the number of
excellent reviews of inserted question literature that
there is certainly more than one correct way to analyze,
synthesize, and evaluate the research literature on
inserted questions. Forced-choice   responses to
higher-order questions may inappropriately limit the
options tot hose of the item writer, testing not the
learner's ability to answer the higher-order question, but
to adapt his or her thinking process to that of the item
writer. The proposed study will use the short-answer,
constructed response mode.

The proposed study will use the short-answer,

Another methodological consideration is the feedback
issue. Does knowledge of the correct response to an
inserted question facilitate learning from the inserted
question? In a survey of the twelve studies he reviewed
that used higher-order questions on the posttest (as the
present study will do), Andre (1979) found that six studies
provided no feedback, one study gave feedback for only part
of the study, another study was unclear regarding feedback
and four studies did provide feedback. It appears that for
lower-order learning, knowledge of the correct response to
adjunct questions results in increased intentional
learning, but not increased incidental learning. Anderson
(1970) cautions, however, that inclusion of correct
responses in a program will not necessarily increase
learning and may impair an adjunct question effect if the
learner pays less attention to answering the question
(Anderson, Kulhavy, and Andre, 1971). Thus, the evidence
relating to this issue is not conclusive. However, it
seems that providing feedback may be facilitative for
inserted questions, providing that conditions are carefully
controlled so that the learner seriously attempts to answer
the inserted question before feedback is provided.

The final methodological consideration is whether a
pretest should be included in the design. A pretest would
allow a more exact calculation learning growth by the
statistical method of residual gain scores. Such a pretest
is not appropriate for inserted question research, though,
because the pretest quite possibly would introduce a
reactive influence. In other words, questions on the
pretest may create a specific attentional effect similar to
that of inserted prequestions (Andre, 1979). This effect
could distort the effects of the treatments.

Learner Aptitudes

The previous section of treatments reported what are
called "main effects," differences between treatment
outcomes that are generally constant for all learners
within a treatment group. When main effects are found, the

practical implication is that one treatment is generally
better than at least one other treatment for all learners
of the type represented in the study sample. Often,
however, educational researchers have failed to find main
effects or discovered only weak ones.

Presence of individual differences among learners or
types of learners has been found to weaken main effects.
When individual differences account for the significant
variability in a study, rather than main effects, the
phenomenon is called aptitude-treatment interaction (ATI)
(Cronbach and Snow, 1977), trait-treatment interaction
(TTI) (Berliner and Cahen, 1973), or attribute-treatment
interaction (ATI) (Tobias, 1976). When
aptitude-by-treatment regression slopes are compared, a
disordinal interaction (when the slopes cross) shows that
one treatment may be more effective for learners within a
given range on the aptitude measure, while another
treatment may benefit learners with a different range on
the aptitude measure. An ordinal reaction (when regression
lines are not parallel, but do not intersect within the
range of observed scores on the variable) shows that one
treatment may be more effective for learners within a given
range on the aptitude measure; at another range, the
treatments are similar in effect.

The within-treatment regression slope shows the
relative performance of subjects varying in amounts of the
measured aptitude. A positive slope indicates that
subjects with high aptitude scores benefit more from that
treatment than students with low aptitude scores; the
inverse is true for a negative slope; a horizontal slope
indicates that students at all aptitude levels benefited
equally by the treatment.

The focus of this section is to determine which
aptitudes (i.e., learner independent variables) might
interact with the treatment components. In addition to
aptitudes that have been shown to interact with inserted
question treatments, consideration will be given to
aptitudes that may interact with video/film media.

Aptitudes and Inserted Questions

Lower-order question studies. Koran and Koran (1972)
studies frequency and spacing of inserted questions. A
significant ATI was obtained for incidental learning: high
verbal-ability learners benefited more than low
verbal-ability learners from treatments of grouped inserted
questions and no questions; higher and lower aptitude
learners benefited equally from the frequent inserted
questions treatment. For associative memory aptitude, high
aptitude learners learned more than low aptitude learners
from both question treatments, while the no question

treatment benefited all learners equally.

Hollen (1970) compared inserted prequestions and postquestions. For associative memory, high aptitude learners gained more than low aptitude learners when using the no question and prequestion treatments. The postquestion treatment, though, showed no advantage for those who remember well.

Examining general intelligence as the aptitude variable, Hershberger (1964) stripped material from a redundant programmed instruction treatment to create a terse version. Each version was presented with and without quiz questions (analogous to inserted questions). With the redundant text, the quiz questions were far more helpful to high general-intelligence subjects than to low general-intelligence subjects; but for the terse text, the no-quiz treatment was better for the high general-intelligence learners, and the quiz treatment was better for low general-intelligence subjects. Thus, the ATI for inserted questions may be dependent on the degree of elaboration in the instructional presentation.

Anderson and Faust (1973) demonstrated that inserted questions have a maximum effect on performance when the subject is operating under low ability or low motivation. In the view of Andre (1979), such students often perceive their task as getting through the material with minimum effort, and therefore the inserted questions direct more of the learners' attention to the information than they would otherwise devote. Conversely, high ability and highly motivated learners may perceive their task to learn as much as possible; therefore, they already devote sufficient attention to the information so that the inserted questions will not significantly increase attention.

A few studies haves investigated ATI for inserted questions in fixed-sequence, fixed-pace media. Levine (1953, reported in Dayton, 1977) found inserted postquestions to be generally facilitating for learners of low motivation, but not for highly motivated learners.

Berliner (1971 and 1972) arrived at inconsistent results in a series of three studies relating memory abilities to learning from televised lectures. It is doubtful, though, that television lectures are comparable to ordinary video/film treatments. Comparing an inserted question treatment to a note-taking treatment to a "pay attention" treatment, he found a significant ATI effect for memory span aptitude on one form of the posttest in experiment one. For subjects high in memory ability, note-taking was a superior treatment to the pay-attention and inserted questions treatments. For low ability subjects, the inserted question treatment was more helpful than the note-taking treatment. An alternate posttest form did not produce any significant ATI. In experiment two, the ATI between note-taking and inserted questions, but not between note-taking and pay-attention, was significant when using the same posttest measure where significance was found in experiment one. Experiment three found no ATI.

Dayton and Schwier (1979) looked for an interaction between Scholastic Aptitude Test (SAT) scores and intentional and incidental learning resulting from treatments of no questions, inserted questions, and grouped inserted questions presented in a slide-tape program. In no case was any interaction found.

Schwier (1979) examined verbal ability and field-dependence/independence as measures of aptitude in a replication of the Dayton and Schwier (1979) study. No significant interactions were demonstrated in this study either.

Higher-order question studies. Again, the most relevant study to this dissertation is the study by Shavelson et al. (1974a). It is the only substantial study of ATIs in the context of higher-order inserted questions ad higher-order outcomes. The aptitudes measured were advanced vocabulary, hidden figures, letter span, memory for semantic implications, and anxiety. Only the advanced vocabulary aptitude interacted significantly with the treatments (higher-order pre and post inserted questions, no questions). Disordinal interactions occurred for both immediate and delayed total and incidental measures. On the immediate total outcomes, for high vocabulary subjects, control and lower-order postquestion treatments were superior to the higher-order postquestion and lower-order prequestion treatments, while for low ability learners, higher-order postquestions were much superior to the other four treatments. On the delayed total outcomes, results were the same as on the immediate outcomes for the low verbal ability learners, but for high ability learners, the lower-order postquestions were significantly superior to the control and higher-order postquestion treatments. Immediate incidental score patterns were quite similar to immediate total score patterns. On the delayed incidental measure, for high verbal ability subjects, the lower-order postquestions were significantly more helpful than higher-order postquestions, and for low ability subjects, the higher-order postquestions were much more beneficial than higher-order prequestions, lower-order postquestions, and lower-order prequestions.

Thus the insertion of the higher-order postquestions appears to aid subjects with low vocabulary scores; generally, lower-order questions were best for students with high vocabulary scores. The results indicate that higher-order postquestions may actually interfere with prose learning for subjects with high verbal comprehension (Andre, 1979). Andre suggests the explanation that high

verbal ability subjects might also be high general ability
subjects who quickly discovered that they could peek ahead
for correct answers provided in the feedback mechanism, and
thus they would not have fully realized the benefit of
inserted questions. These findings can be contrasted with
findings by Koran and Koran (1972) who found that
lower-order inserted questions benefited equally students
who were high and low in verbal comprehension. Overall the
findings are consistent with the findings of Rothkopf
(1972) and Anderson and Faust (1973) reported earlier.

Aptitudes and Video/Film

     If vocabulary aptitude interacts significantly with
inserted question treatments to affect learning from prose,
a measure of video/film literacy (the ability to decode the
"vocabulary" and "language" of video and film) might also
interact with inserted questions to affect learning from
video/film. Vocabulary and video/film literacy may be
corresponding aptitudes for the two media. Perhaps
students with low measures of video/film literacy might
benefit from inserted questions the same way that low
verbal ability students benefit from inserted questions in
prose.
     While numerous vocabulary measures have been developed
and validated, few video/film literacy measures have been
similarly developed. Not much has changed since Pryluck
and Snow (1967, p.54) asserted that there were "few terms,
categories, or propositions available for analyzing the
syntactical and semantic characteristics of the [film]
message." The purpose of this section of the literature
review is to identify measures that might provide a direct
or indirect indicator of video/film literacy aptitude.
     First, though, it will be useful to briefly discuss the
background of the video/film literacy construct. Hoban and
Van Ormer (1959) held that motion pictures consisted of a
system of conventions, a "language" used by film makers and
understood by audiences. This audience understanding
provides a simple definition of the term "film literacy."
The concept embraces the ability to decode the symbolic
codes or grammars unique to film and te vision (Salomon,
1974). Pryluck and Snow (1967, p. 56 escribed some of
the grammatical elements:

          Gradually, the rhetoric of motion
          pictures was increasingly differentiated
          from stage productions, using the unique
          capacity of motion pictures to collapse
          time and space through editing and
          photography. In less than a generation,
          the outline of most of the conventions

had been established: intercutting
parallel story lines that converge at a
climax; shifting the camera viewpoint to
include close-ups, extremely long shots,
and the whole range between; the dolly
shot which facilitate fluid photographic
composition, etc.

Add to these elements slow motion, zoom shots, rotations,
logical gaps, fragmented spaces, fades, dissolves, etc.
The latest refinement of the video/film literacy construct
is that of Salomon and Cohen (1978): the mental handling of
codes which leads to the extraction of knowledge from coded
messages, that is, skillful decoding. It is an aptitude
for comprehending video/film, much the same as verbal
aptitude relates to the language of words.

Pryluck and Snow (1967) credit Ruesch and Kees (1956)
with introducing a classification system which further
clarifies the semantic and grammatical elements of
video/film: digital and analogic information. Digital
information consists of letters, words, numbers, and other
familiar symbols which are serial and discrete; it unfolds
across a page, lecture, or screen one unit at a time.
Digital data are symbols with conventionalized significance
and no relationship to their referent. Analogic
information is composed of pictures, gestures, intonations,
etc. It is simultaneous and continuous and is capable of
conveying in a single instant a wide range of continuously
changing information. Thus video/film can be analyzed into
six subdivisions of digital and analogic information:
digital channels are (1) audio verbal and (2) video verbal;
analogic channels are (3) audio nonverbal and (4) video
nonverbal, and (5) audio paraverbal and (6) video
paraverbal.

The question, then, is how might a subject's ability to
interpret these video/film communication components be
measured? a few studies have employed measures that may
directly or indirectly relate to this ability.

The most direct attempts to measure this construct are
a series of film and audio tests developed by Seibert,
Reid, and Snow (1967) and Seibert and Snow (1965).
Unfortunately most of these measures were never developed
beyond an experimental stage; but one index, a test for
"film memory," has been employed in a number of studies on
learning (e.g., Koran, Snow, and McDonald, 1971). Snow
(Note2) describes the test as a rather crude measure, but
one better than other film literacy measures currently
available to study college students. Simply, it tests the
subject's recall of a very short film's rendition of a
sequence of events taking place on a street.

Other studies have employed measures that may provide
indirect indexes of video/film aptitude. It may be, for

example, that experience with video/film would positively correlate with video/film literacy. VanderMeer (1950) demonstrated that ninth graders who had been exposed to a series of 44 films in a general science course learned more from a series of geography and natural-history films than their peers who had not been exposed to the general science films.

Snow, Tiffen, and Seibert (1965) executed one of the early formal ATI studies on learning by means of a filmed physics lecture demonstration. They found that students with high scores on measures of attitude toward instructional films, past experience with entertainment films, and past experience with instructional films gained more from this filmed demonstration than students scoring low on these three measures.

The validity of these scales to measure the construct of video/film literacy is unproved. All of these scales that have demonstrated at least some positive relationship to learning via film will be used in the proposed study. These four scales are necessary because no single index is clearly more valid than the other.

Summary

Inserted question research has investigated intentional and incidental learning, higher-order and lower-order learning, and immediate and delayed learning. The findings indicate that higher-order and lower-order inserted postquestions can significantly benefit both intentional and incidental learning, especially from prose.

In prose studies, students of high verbal ability seem to benefit much more from lower-order postquestions than higher-order questions, while the inverse seems to be true for students of low verbal ability.

Inserted question effects have been studies for lower-order questions in video/film, but not for higher-order questions.

Video/film literacy may be related to learning from video in a similar way to the relationship of verbal ability to learning from prose. Measures of film memory, attitude toward instructional film, and experience with TV/film entertainment may provide indirect indexes of video/film literacy.

It is appropriate in research on learning from inserted higher- and lower-order questions in video to include the adjunct questions directly in the video production; to ask adjunct questions requiring short-answer, constructive responses; and to provide follow-up feedback response to the inserted question.

METHOD

Research Design

The basic design of the proposed study is patterned
after the 1974 study by Shavelson, Berliner, Ravitch, and
Loeding, "Effects of Position and Type of Question on
Learning from Prose Material: Interaction of Treatments
with Individual Differences." The major changes from this
study will be the substitution of videotape and the mode of
information presentation, the deletion of question position
as a treatment factor, and the substitution of some
different aptitudes for examination of ATI effects.

The research design is a posttest-only, control group,
factorial experiment (Campbell and Stanley, 1963), modified
by the addition of an ATI component. The design is shown
below:

Attribute Variables	Treatment	Immediate Posttest	Delayed Posttest
X_{1-7}	T_1	Y_1	Y_2
X_{1-7}	T_2	Y_1	Y_2
X_{1-7}	T_3	Y_1	Y_2

Approximately two weeks before the treatment
intervention, the subjects will be measured on selected
aptitudes. For the treatment sessions, the students will
be randomly assigned to one of three treatment groups and
will meet simultaneously in similar, but separate locations
to view the videotape and take an immediate posttest. Two
to three weeks later the same posttest will be given as a
delayed measure as part of a regular course examination
(e.g., midterm or final). At a later date, the researcher
will report a summary of the results of the study to
members of the class.

Treatments

Subjects will be randomly assigned to one of three
treatment groups: videotape presentation only (V),
videotape with higher-order inserted postquestions (VH),
and videotape with lower-order inserted postquestions

(VL). Each group will meet simultaneously in separate but similar studios The subjects will be informed that the videotape which they are about to see contains material for the course they are taking and that the scores they earn on the tests of the videotape content will count toward their course grade. The two inserted-question treatment groups will be directed to write answers to the questions contained in the videotape that will be screened for each group. Subjects will not be told that the answer sheets will be collected until the videotape presentation is completed. After the answer sheets are collected, an immediate posttest will be administered.

Those versions with inserted postquestions will contain a total of five questions of the respective treatment level edited into the tape. Five different "naturally" occurring breaks in the tape content, approximately every three minutes, will be selected; and a question will be inserted in each break. The questions will be edited into the tape from a character generator which will type alphanumeric characters onto the screen. A voiceover will read the question, direct the students to write their answers on the provided answer sheet, and inform the subjects how much time they will be given to compose their answers (short, open-ended, constructed responses).

Lower-order inserted postquestions will reflect the knowledge level of Bloom's taxonomy, encompassing recall of specifics, recall of ways and means of dealing with specifics, and recall of universals and abstractions in the field. Sources of the answers to these questions will be representative of both verbal-audio videotape content and video and audio nonverbal paraverbal content (Ruesch and Kees, 1956).

Higher-order inserted postquestions will address the application, analysis, and evaluation levels of the taxonomy. The comprehension (second) level of the taxonomy will not be included so as to provide a clear distinction between higher- and lower-order processes; the synthesis level will not be considered because previous research on inserted questions provides no precedent for its use here. Like the lower-order treatment, questions at each higher-cognitive level will be answerable both by verbal audio sources of videotape content and by sources of video and audio nonverbal and paraverbal videotape content. The higher-order questions will focus on the same portions of content as specified by the lower-order questions; that is, the same knowledge called for by the VL questions will form the basis for ultimately answering the VH questions. The matched sets of lower-order and higher-order adjunct questions will be asked at identical break points in the videotape.

The inserted questions will be constructed jointly by the course professor and the researcher. They will be

examined for the face validity of the cognitive level and
of the video/film channel elements by independent
specialists in question analysis, video/film theory, and
measurement and testing.

The inserted question will remain on the screen the
entire time. After the time allotted to answer a question
has elapsed, and answer will be provided via the character
generator. For the VL treatment, a sample correct answer
will be offered. The voiceover will explain why the answer
is correct and will direct the students to compare their
own responses to the answer provided on the screen. In the
VH treatment, the voiceover will clarify that the sample
answer is not necessarily the only correct answer.

The sequence for the three treatments is compared in
Table 2.

Table 2. Design Sequence
_____

| VH Group | VL Group | V Group (control) |

2 weeks before treatment session, all students measured for
aptitudes

1. random
    assignment
	1. random
	    assignment
		1. random
		    assignment

2. treatment
   a. view video-
      tape section
   b. answer higher-
      order postQ
   c. compare own
      answer to
      sample
      corrected
      answer
   d. recycle a-c
      for remaining
      sections
	2. treatment
	   a. view video-
	      tape section
	   b. answer lower
	      order postQ
	   c. compare own
	      answer to
	      sample
	   d. recycle a-c
	      for remaing
	      sections
		2. treatment:
		      view entire
		      videotape,
		      uninterrupted

3. submit VH answer
   sheet
	3. submit VL answer
	   sheet	

4. immediate
   posttest
	4. immediate
	   posttest
		4. immediate
		   posttest

_____
2-3 weeks after treatment, delayed posttest in regular
course exam.

To prevent contamination among the three treatment
groups between the completion of the immediate posttest and
the delayed posttest, students will be told not to discuss

the videotape session until after the experiment has been concluded. Also, no further formal instruction or discussion will be included in the course regarding the videotape content and the inserted questions. Nor will the differences in the treatments be discussed in the course until after the delayed posttest.

Subjects

A large class (N=200 or more) of university undergraduate students (e.g., a general psychology course) at the University of _____ will represent the college/university population. Most likely the course will be one which meets general graduation requirements. Thus the distribution of the enrollees will be fairly representative of university undergraduates in terms of general intelligence and other aptitudes, gender, socioeconomic status, attitudes, experience, etc. Students will be randomly assigned to one of the three treatment groups.

Independent Measures

General Intelligence and Verbal Aptitude. Students will be asked to release permission to the researcher for access to their SAT or ACT scores on file with the university. These scores will be converted to standardized z scores to produce a common index for all subjects. The total score will estimate the students' general intelligence, and the verbal subtest score will represent their verbal aptitude.

SAT or ACT measures are required in the university's application process. Their validity and reliability have been well established through their development over many years with hundreds of thousands of high school senior subjects throughout the United States. Internal reliability for the American College Testing (ACT) Assessment is approximately .90, and for the Scholastic Aptitude Test (SAT) of the College Board, approximately .91. The correlation between the SAT and ACT measures is approximately .88 (Rankin, Note 3), almost as high as the internal reliabilities for each of the two measures.

Content Area Ability. An investigation of how individual differences interact with film on learning by Snow, Tiffen, and Seibert (1965) demonstrated the significant influence of prior knowledge of the content area being learned (physics). The present study will use the subject's total raw score on the course final examination as a measurement of this construct.

Film Memory. A measure of film memory was developed by
Seibert, Reid, and Snow (1967). Its use in the Koran,
Snow, and McDonald (1971) study demonstrated an interaction
with the film instructional treatments. Snow (Note 2)
characterized this test as an index of the subject's
ability to recall spatial and temporal sequences presented
in a short silent film of events taking place on a city
street. This measure will be used in the present study.

Attitude toward Instructional TV/Film. The study by
Snow, Tiffen, and Seibert (1965) also found an interaction
involving learning from film and a measure of attitude
toward instructional film. Their scale will be used in the
current study.

Experiences with TV/Film Instruction and TV/Film
Entertainment. Both of these experience variables were
shown in the Snow, Tiffen, and Seibert study to interact
with film learning. Simple inventories of both
instructional and non-instructional TV/film experience will
be developed by the researcher. These inventories will be
patterned after the Snow, Tiffen, and Seibert measures, but
adjusted for changes in experience level of the public from
1965 to 1980.

Dependent Measures

The same posttest will be used for both the immediate
outcome measure and for the delayed measure. While the
posttest will be administered as a single instrument, it
will include four scales to measure: (1) higher-order
intentional learning, (2) lower-order intentional learning,
(3) higher-order incidental learning, and (4) lower-order
incidental learning.

Intentional Learning. Items composing the higher-order
intentional scale will be the five higher-order adjunct
questions in the VH treatment. The lower-order scale will
be composed of the five VL inserted questions.
A difficulty in equating scores on the higher-order and
lower-order scales is acknowledged. That is, the
higher-order intentional scale is really an intentional
scale for only the VH treatment group, and likewise the
lower-order intentional scale is really a valid measure of
intentional learning for only the VL group. Thus a direct
comparison between the score of the VH group on its true
intentional scale and the score of the VL group on its true
intentional scale is not possible. Rather, two independent
comparisons will be made, one for how the VH group differed
from the other two treatment groups in performance on the

higher-order intentional scale questions, and likewise a comparison of how the VL scores differed from those of the other two groups on the lower-order intentional scale questions.

Incidental Learning. This investigation defines incidental learning as the ability to answer questions over the content of the information presentation not tested by intentional questions. Again, both higher-order and lower-order scales will result. The questions will be similar in format to the intentional questions, but will require answers based on different content from the content covered by the intentional questions. An attempt will be made for the content providing the basis for the answers to the lower-order questions to be the same as that for the higher-order questions.

Summary

Each posttest, immediate and delayed, will be composed of 20 questions: 5 higher-order questions for both intentional and incidental learning, and 5 lower-order questions for both intentional and incidental learning, and 5 lower-order questions for both intentional and incidental learning. Just as for the treatment questions, the posttest questions will have their answers based both on verbal audio information in the videotape and information transmitted by nonverbal or paraverbal audio or video content. All questions will be answered by short, constructed responses. Like the treatment questions, all posttest questions will be developed jointly by the researcher and the course professor to ensure content validity. The same evaluations regarding question level and information source mode that are used for the treatment questions will be employed for posttest questions as well. Each student will earn a score for four learning scales: (1) higher-order intentional learning, (2) lower-order intentional learning, (3) higher-order incidental learning, and (4) lower-order incidental learning.

Data Analysis

Reliability of New Instruments. Except for the SAT and ACT measures, all instruments used in this study will be evaluated for internal reliability by Tryon's General Case Reliability formula.

Intercorrelation between Measures. An analysis of the correlation between scores on the independent measure scores will be done to determine the extent to which they are measuring the same factors. Also to be examined will be the correlation of scores on the various learning scales within the respective treatment groups.

Main and Interaction Effects. Multiple regression will be used to determine the amount of variance on a particular posttest variable explained by (1) each aptitude, (2) each treatment, and (3) interaction between aptitudes and treatments.

Human Relations

The students will be advised that the course professor has given permission to conduct this study in this course, that the course professor is participating in the design of the treatments and tests, and the the tests will contribute to the course grade of each student. The students will be requested to provide cooperation, and a form will be signed (with the student's ID number) by those students who will release access to their SAT or ACT scores on file with the University for the purpose of this study.

All raw data will be kept in full confidence by the researcher. Students' scores on the delayed posttest will be released to the course professor. Otherwise all scores will be treated in a coded format separate from the student's name.

The dissertation and any other subsequent reporting of this study will present only summarized data.

Timeline for Proposed Study

Time Period	Activity
April	Select dissertation committee Formal proposal review Locate course sample for project
May	Select appropriate film or videotape Develop new aptitude measures Develop treatments and posttest
June 01-13	Validate new aptitude measures Validate all treatments and posttest
June 18	Administer aptitude measures Randomly assign subjects to treatments
June 19	Administer treatments and immediate posttest

July 03	Administer delayed posttest
June 23-July 14	Compute results
June 30-July 18	Analyze results
July 21-Aug. 01	Write rough draft of dissertation chapters 4 and 5
August	Complete dissertation for formal review Write abstract Orally defend dissertation

BIBILIOGRAPHY

Reference Notes

[1]Berliner, David C. Personal communication via telephone, February 19, 1980.
[2]Snow, Richard E. Personal communication via telephone, February 16, 1980.
[3]Rankin, Richard J. Personal communication, April 11, 1980.

References

Allen, D.I. Some effects of advance organizers and level of questions on the learning and retention of written social studies material. Journal of Educational Psychology, 1970, 61, 333-339.

Anderson, R.C. Control of student mediating processes during verbal learning and instruction. Review of Educational Research, 1970, 40, 349-369.

Anderson R.C., and Biddle, W.B. On asking people questions about what they are reading. In G. Bower (Ed.), Psychology of learning and motivation (Vol. 9). New York: Academic Press, 1975.

Anderson R.C. and Faust, G. W. The effects of strong formal prompts in programmed instruction. American Educational Research Journal, 1967, 4, 345-352.

Anderson, R.C., Kulhavy, R.W., and Andre, R. Feedback procedures in programmed instruction. Journal of Educational Psychology, 1971, 62 148-156.

Andre, T. Does answering higher-level questions while reading facilitate productive learning? Review of Educational Research, 1979, 49, 280-318.

Andre, T. The role of paraphrased and verbatim adjunct questions in facilitating learning by reading. Paper presented at the annual meeting of the Midwestern Educational Research Association, Bloomingdale, IL., 1978.

Andre, T. Learning concepts from prose. Final report grant 406-21-01. Ames, IA: Iowas State University, 1976.

Andre, T., and Sola, J. Imagery, verbatim and paraphrased
    questions and retention of meaningful sentences.
    Journal of Educational Psychology, 1976, 68, 661-669.

Andre, T., and Womack, S. Verbatim and paraphrased adjunct
    questions learning from prose. Journal of Educational
    Psychology, 1978, 70, 796-802.

Berliner, D.C. The generalizability of aptitude-treatment
    Interactions across subject matter. Paper presented at
    the meeting of the American Educational Research
    Association, Chicago, IL, April, 1972.

Berliner, D.C. Aptitude-treatment interactions in two
    studies of learning from lecture instruction. Paper
    presented at the meeting of the American Educational
    Research Association, New York, February, 1971.

Berliner, D.C. and Cahen, L.S. Trait-treatment
    interaction and learning. Review of Research in
    Education, 1973, 1, 58-94.

Bloom, B. S. (Ed.). Taxonomy of educational objectives:
    The classification of educational goals, handbook I:
    cognitive domain, New York: David McKay, 1956.

Boker, J.R. Immediate and delayed retention effects of
    interspersing questions in written instructional
    passages. Journal of Educational Psychology, 1974, 66,
    96-98.

Campbell, T., and Stanley, J.C. Experimental and
    quasi-experimental designs for research on teaching.
    In N.L. Gage (Ed.), Handbook of Research on Teaching.
    Chicago: Rank McNally, 1963.

Cronbach, L.J. and Snow, R. E. Aptitudes and
    instructional methods: A handbook for research on
    interactions. New York: Irvington, 1977.

Dapra, R.A., and Felker, D.B. Effects of comprehension and
    verbatim adjunct questions on problem-solving ability
    from prose material: Extension of the mathemagenic
    hypothesis. Paper presented at the annual convention
    of the American Psychological Association, New Orleans,
    1974.

Dayton, D.K. Inserted postquestions and learning from
    slide-tape presentations: Implications of the
    mathemagenic hypothesis. AV Communication Review,
    1977, 25, 125-146.

Dayton, D.K., and Schwier, R.A. Effects of postquestions on learning and learning efficiency from fixed-pace, fixed-sequence media. _Educational Communication and Technology--a Journal of Theory, Research, and Development_, 1979, _27_, 103-113.

Dewey, J. _How we think_. Lexington, MA: Raytheon/Heath, 1933.

Distand, H.W. A study of the reading performance of pupils under different conditions on different types of materials. _Journal of Educational Psychology_, 1927, _18_, 247-258.

Fitch, J.G. _Lectures on teaching_, New York: Kellog, 1879.

Frase, L.T. Some unpredicted effects of different questions on learning from connected discourse. _Journal of Educational Psychology_, 1968, _59_, 266-272.

Frase, L.T. Effects of question location, pacing, and mode upon retention of prose material. _Journal of Educational Psychology_, 1968, _59_, 244-249. (b)

Frase, L.T. Learning from prose material: Length of passage, knowledge of results and position of questions. _Journal of Educational Psychology_, 1967, _58_, 266-272.

Frase, L.T., Patrick, E.M., and Schumer, H. Effect of question position and frequency upon learning from text under different levels of incentive. _Journal of Educational Psychology_, 1970, _61_, 52-56.

Gagne, R.M. _The conditions of learning_, 2nd ed. New York: Holt, Rinehard and Winston, 1970.

Gall, M.D., Ward, B.A., Berliner, D.C., Cahen, L.S., Winne, P.H., Edashoff, J.D., and Stanton, G.C. Effects of questioning techniques and recitation on student learning. _American Educational Research Journal_, 1978, _15_, 175-199.

Germane, C.E. The value of the controlled mental summary as a method of studying. _School and Society_, 1920, _12_, 591-593.

Heestand, D.E. _The effects of inserted postquestions and individual differences on learning from two videotape programs_. Unpublished doctoral dissertation, Indiana University, 1979.

Hershberger, W. Self-evaluation responding and typographical cueing. _Journal of Educational Psychology_, 1964, _55_, 288-296.

Hoban, C.F., and Van Ormer, E.B. _Instructional film research (rapid mass learning) 1918-1915_. Technical Report SCD 269-7-19. Port Washington, NY: Navy Special Devices Center, 1959.

Hollen, T.T. _Interaction of individual abilities with the presence and position of adjunct questions in learning from prose materials._ Unpublished doctoral dissertation, University of Texas, 1970.

Holley, C.E. _The teacher's technique_. New York: Century, 1923.

Holmes, E. Reading guided by questions versus careful reading and rereading without questions. _School Review_, 1931, _39_, 361-371.

Joyce, B., and Weil, M. _Models of teaching_. Englewood Cliffs, NJ: Prentice-Hall, 1972.

Kantor, B.R. Effectiveness of inserted questions in instructional films. _AV Communication Review_, 1960, _8_, 104-108.

Koran, M.L. and Koran, J.J., Jr. _Differential response to question pacing in learning from prose_. Paper presented to American Educational Research Association, 1972.

Koran, M.L., Snow, R.E., and McDonald, F.J. Teacher aptitude and observational learning of a teaching skill. _Journal of Educational Psychology_, 1971, _62_, 219-228.

Levine, S. The role of motivation in t he effects of "active review" on learning from a factual film. (Abstract) _The American Psychologist_, 1953, _8_, 388-389.

McGaw, B. and Grotelueschen, A. Direction of the effect of questions in prose material. _Journal of Educational Psychology_, 1972, _63_, 580-588.

McKenzie, G.R. Some effects of frequent quizzes on inferential thinking. _American Educational Research Journal_, 1972, _9_, 231-240.

May, M.A., Lumsdaine, A.A., and Hadsell, R.S. Questions spliced into a film for motivation and pupil participation. In May, M.A. and Lumsdaine, A.A. Learning from films. New Haven, CN: Yale University Press, 1958.

Michael, D.N., and Maccoby, N. Factors influencing verbal learning from films under varying conditions of audience participation. Journal of Experimental Psychology, 1953, 46, 411-418.

Moore, W.D. The control of learning through the use of different types of testlike events. Paper presented at the annual meeting of the American Educational Research Association, Washington, D.C., 1975.

Pryluck, C., and Snow, R.E. Toward a psycholinquistics of cinema. AV Communication Review, 1967, 15, 54-75.

Rickards, J.P. Adjunct postquestions in text: A critical review of methods and processes. Review of Educational Research, 1979, 49, 181-196.

Rickards, J.P., and DiVesta, F.J. Type and frequency of questions in processing textual material. Journal of Educational Psychology, 1974, 66, 354-362.

Rothkopf, E.Z. Writing to teach and reading to learn: A perspective on the psychology of written instruction. In N.L. Gage (Ed.), The psychology of teaching methods. Chicago: The National Society for the study of education, 1976.

Rothkopf, E.Z. Variable adjunct question schedules, interpersonal interaction, and incidental learning form written material. Journal of Educational Psychology, 1972, 63, 87-92.

Rothkopf, E.Z. The concept of mathemagenic activities. Review of Educational Research, 1970, 40, 325-336.

Rothkopf, E.Z. Learning from written instructive material: An exploration of the control of inspection behavior by test-like events. American Educational Research Journal, 1966, 3, 241-249.

Rothkopf, E.Z. Some conjectures about inspection behavior in learning from written sentences and the response made problem in programmed self-instruction. Journal of Programmed Instruction, 1963, 2, 31-45.

Rothkopf, E.Z., and Bisbicos, E.E. Selective facilitative effects of interspersed questions on learning from written materials. Journal of Educational Psychology, 1967, 58, 56-61.

Rothkopf, E.Z., and Bloom, R.D. Effects of interpersonal interaction on the instructional value of adjunct questions in learning from written material. Journal of Educational Psychology, 1970, 61, 417-422.

Salomon, G. Internalization of filmic operation in relation to individual differences. Journal of Educational Psychology, 1974, 66, 499-511.

Salomon, G., and Cohen, A.A. On the meaning and validity of television viewing. Human Communication Research, 1978, 4, 265-270.

Schwier, R.A. The effect of individual differences and inserted postquestions upon learning from slide-tape presentations. Unpublished doctoral dissertation, Indiana University, 1979.

Seibert, W.F., Reid, C., and Snow, R.E. Studies in cine-psychometry II. (Final Report, U.S. Office of Education, 7-24-0880-257) Lafayette, IN: Purdue University, Audio-Visual Center, 1965.

Seibert, W.F., and Snow, R.E. Cine-psychometry. AV Communication Review, 1965, 13, 140-158.

Shavelson, R.J., Berliner, D.C., Ravitch, M.M., and Loeding, D. Effects of Position and type of question on learning from prose material: Interaction of treatments with individual differences. Journal of Educational Psychology, 1974, 66, 40-48. (a)

Shavelson, R.J., Berliner, D.C., Loeding, D., Porteus, A.W., and Stanton, G.C. Adjunct questions mathemagenics, and mathemathanics. Paper presented at the annual meeting of the American Psychological Association, New Orleans, 1974.

Snow, R.E.; Tiffin, J.; and Seibert, W.F. Individual differences and instructional film effects. Journal of Educational Psychology, 1965, 56, 315-326.

Teather, D.C.B., and Marchant, H. Particular reference to the effects of cueing, questioning, and knowledge of results. Programmed Learning and Educational Technology, 1974, 11, 317-327.

Tobias, S. Achievement treatment interactions. Review of Educational Research, 1976, 46, 61-74.

Tyack, D.B. The one best system: A history of American urban education. Cambridge, MA: Harvard University Press, 1974.

VanderMeer, A.W. Systems analysis and media--a perspective. AV Communication Review, 1964. 12, 292-301.

Vuke, G.J. Effects of inserted questions in films on developing an understanding of controlled experimentation. Unpublished doctoral dissertation, Indiana University, 1962.

Washbourne, J.N. The use of prequestions in social science material. Journal of Educational Psychology, 1929, 20, 321-354.

Watts, G.H. Effects of prequestions on control of attention in written instruction. The Australian Journal of Education, 1973, 18, No. 1.

Watts, G.H., and Anderson, R.C. Effects of three types of inserted questions on learning from prose. Journal of Educational Psychology, 1971, 62, 387-394.

Woods, A. and Andre, T. Level of adjunct question, type of feedback, and learning concepts from prose. Paper presented at the annual meeting of the American Educational Research Association, Toronto, Canada, 1978.

Philip C. Mendel

Dissertation Proposal

An Investigation of Factors That Influence Teacher
Morale and Satisfaction with Work Conditions

Information about the completed dissertation is in
Dissertation Abstracts International, vol. 48, no. 11,
section A, page 2779. The DAI order number is DA 880538

INTRODUCTION

Purpose of the Study 巴川1.

The major purpose of this study is to identify factors that affect teacher morale and satisfaction with work conditions. Morale is defined here as the teacher's feeling state about his or her work situation as a whole, whereas satisfaction is defined as the teacher's feeling state about specific aspects of the work situation.

Specifically, the study will determine whether teachers' level of satisfaction and level of morale are influenced by their ethnicity, sex, age, college training, teaching assignment, teacher classification, and years of teaching experience. Also, the study will determine whether a teacher's perceived level of morale is affected by satisfaction with work conditions.

A related purpose of the study is to determine the status of teacher morale on Guam and to identify working conditions with which teachers are satisfied or dissatisfied.

The particular teacher group to be studied is the public school teachers on Guam during the 1986-87 school year.

Background

I could not find a widely accepted definition of morale or satisfaction in my review of literature. I will present definitions of morale found in studies and will discuss their common elements. I will then present a definition for satisfaction and show how researchers have used two terms interchangeably. Finally, I will define morale and satisfaction as used in this study.

Definition of Moral and Satisfaction. Ramsey (1984) defined morale as "the way employees felt about themselves, their work place, and their overall working life." The Dictionary of Education (Good, 1973) defines teacher morale as the "collective feelings and attitudes of a teacher group as related to their duties, responsibilities, goals, supervisors, and fellow workers." Bentley and Rempel (1980), developers of a measure of morale (the Purdue Teacher Opinionaire), defined morale as "the professional interest and enthusiasm that a person displays towards the achievement of individual and group goals in a given job situation." Andrew, Parks, and Nelson (1985) defined morale as "a subjective phenomenon, experienced by each member of a group in an individual way... and is ... a feeling that pervades the spirit of a group."

A common element in the terms described above is the overall, global feeling that a worker feels toward the workable environment. Therefore, for purposes of this study, I will define morale as "the general feeling state of teachers towards their overall work environment." Morale will be measured by a single item asking teachers to rate their level of morale.

I found in my review of research that researchers have used the terms "morale" and "satisfaction" interchangeably. The American Heritage Dictionary (Berube, 1982) defines satisfaction as "the fulfillment or gratification of a desire or need." Gorton (1976) stated that "both employee satisfaction and morale are attitudinal variables that reflect positive or negative feelings about particular persons or situations." He noted that the two terms often are used synonymously in educational literature. Murphy (1985) defined the term job satisfaction as "the positive attitude of teachers toward their jobs," but does not use the term morale. In his study of morale, Frese (1984) defined morale but did not differentiate it from satisfaction.

For purposes of this study, I will define satisfaction as "the positive feeling or attitude a teacher has toward a particular worksite condition." In other words, I consider "satisfaction" to reflect a more limited attitude than "morale." Worksite conditions involve a variety of elements, including: the principal, the teaching environment, the teaching staff, salary, workload, the curriculum, teacher status, community support of education, community pressures, and school facilities and services. Satisfaction will be measured in this study by the Purdue Teacher Opinionaire because it has differentiated scales measuring the teachers' attitude toward these worksite conditions.

Why is Teacher Morale Important? For the past three decades, researchers have been interested in identifying the effects of work morale and satisfaction on worker productivity. Initial studies were done in industry and later replicated in educational institutions.

The classic study on worksite satisfaction in industry was done by Herzberg, Mausner, and Snyderman (1959). They studied two hundred engineers and accountants and found that productivity was positively related to job satisfaction and high morale.

Miller (1981) concluded from his study that "the morale of the staff can have a positive effect on pupil attitudes and learning. Raising the teacher morale level is not only making teaching more pleasant for teachers, buy also learning more pleasant for the students. This creates an environment that is more conducive to learning." Hansford (1961) discovered, "Where morale was high, schools showed an increase in student achievement, and therefore, were much better schools than those where morale levels were low." In a recent study of 36 organizations, Oldham and Hackman (1981) found that work performance was closely related to satisfaction or dissatisfaction of employees.

Additional effects of dissatisfaction and low morale might include stress and burnout. Kirk and Walter (1981) concluded that low morale leads to teacher burnout, which subsequently causes teachers to drop out of the profession or to experience mental health problems. Burnout as defined by Maslach (1978) is emotional exhaustion caused by job stress and is a product of low morale. Indicators of burnout as listed by Walsh (1979) include a loss of concern for and detachment from the people with whom one works, decreased quality of teaching, depression, greater use of sick leave, efforts to leave the profession, and a cynical and dehumanized perception of students.

In summary, there is some research evidence that satisfied teachers are more productive than dissatisfied ones. Teacher morale affects student learning, the health of the organization, and the health of the teacher.

That satisfied employees are more productive has important implications for educational administration. It means that administrators should be concerned with teachers' morale and satisfaction because these conditions have a significant bearing on educational productivity. The proposed study will examine factors that are related to teacher morale and satisfaction. The assumption is that these factors may indirectly affect educational productivity through their effect on teacher morale and satisfaction.

What Factors Influence Teacher Morale? Numerous studies have been conducted to determine factors that affect morale and satisfaction. A National Education Association Survey (NEA, 1980) identified five factors that negatively affect teacher job satisfaction: (1) public attitudes toward the schools, (2) treatment of education by the media, (3) student attitudes toward learning, (4) salary, and (5) status of teachers in the community.

Pagel and Price (1980) studied 130 teachers and found that their job dissatisfaction was caused by the following factors: (1) lack of planning time, (2) tedious paper and clerical work, (3) an out-of-touch and autocratic administration, (4) disruptive and unmotivated students, (5) non-teaching activities, such as faculty meetings and "time-wasting" workshops, (6) uncooperative parents, (7) lack of autonomy to prescribe curricula, (8) feelings of failure, and (9) low occupational prestige. Kirk and Walter (1981) discovered that "feelings of isolation, loneliness, and lack of support contributed to low teacher morale."

Duncan (1976) found that teacher morale was significantly higher in schools with employee-oriented administrators than in schools with task-oriented administrators.

A Lou Harris (1984) survey of public school teachers across the nation in June 1984 found that fifty-two percent were dissatisfied with the respect shown to teachers by society. "Public attitudes toward schools and treatment of education by the mass media are reported by teachers to be the number one and number two variables contributing to job dissatisfaction," stated Feistritzer (1983).

Ford (1979) reported dissatisfaction can result from variable workloads. Miskel and others (1972) found that factors contributing to teacher satisfaction included intrinsic job variables such as achievement, recognition, work itself, responsibility, and advancement. They also found that teacher dissatisfaction was caused by extrinsic factors such as salary, possibilities for growth, interpersonal relations with subordinates, status, interpersonal relations with superiors, interpersonal relations with peers, policy and administration, working conditions, personal life, and job security.

Promotional opportunities seem important to teachers. Lowther, Gill, and Copard (1982) noted dissatisfaction by teachers who feel they are locked in vertically as well as horizontally and, unlike many other workers, are denied the opportunity for promotion even when their performance is outstanding.

Merit pay has been mentioned by several educators as the most controversial topic of studies involving teacher satisfaction and dissatisfaction. Bruno and Nottingham (1978) argued that merit pay is the best means for improving the satisfaction of teachers and proposed a complicated incentive scheme to reward teachers with some precision according to student performance. Meyer (1975f) and Deci (1975) both condemned merit pay plans because they "embody a basic condescension, promote unhealthy competition, threaten self-esteem, and weaken intrinsic motivation because such plans carry the potential to cheapen education and subvert teachers' service ethic." A review of research conducted at the National Institute of Education, Washington, D.C. (1981), revealed that money may not be the best way to motivate teachers, because they appear to be more influenced by the intrinsic rewards of teaching. The research pointed most emphatically to a single conclusion about merit pay: its potential rewards are uncertain and it should be adopted with a good deal of care.

Meyer (1975) advocated a promotional system as a substitute for merit pay plans because most management theorists find advancement to be a more potent motivator than money.

In summary, factors that have been found to influence teacher satisfaction and morale include: public attitudes toward the school, salary, teacher status, treatment of education by media, student attitudes toward learning, lack of planning time, tedious paper and clerical work, non-teaching activities, uncooperative parents, achievement, recognition, work itself, responsibility, and advancement. Other factors are salary, possibilities of growth, interpersonal relations with superiors or peers, policy and administration, working conditions, personal life, job security, promotional opportunities, and merit pay.

The instrument to be used in this study will measure many of these factors, specifically, public attitudes toward school, salary, teacher status, tedious paper and clerical work, the job itself, interpersonal relations with superiors, interpersonal relations with peers, policy and administration, and working conditions.

School principals and other administrators need to know the factors that have a positive or negative effect on teacher satisfaction and morale. Knowledge of these factors may assist them in making better decisions about interventions to improve teacher morale and satisfaction.

What Is Teachers' Level of Satisfaction and Morale?

The level of morale of the teaching population on Guam is worth assessing for several reasons. The ethnic composition to Guam teachers in unlike that of any group of teachers to be found in a mainland school district. A majority (63.2%) of the public school teachers are Chamorros and indigenous to the island. Slightly over thirty percent of the teachers are persons who have traveled thousands of miles to join the public school system -- Filipinos (15.7%) who journeyed some 1,500 miles eastward from their Asian homeland, or U.S. mainlanders (15.9%) who traveled west some 3,000 to 8,000 miles to teach on America's western-most Pacific possession.

The teaching workforce on Guam faces environmental conditions unlike those found in a stateside community. A large number of island residents are employed by the U.S. Navy and U.S. Air Force, which operate various military support facilities on the island. The local business community focuses on trade resulting from several hundred thousand tourists from Japan who visit this "piece of America," which is so near to Japan. There is no local industry to speak of. If any teachers in the system become dissatisfied to the point of wanting to relocate to a U.S. school district, they have to move some 3,000 miles to Hawaii, or an additional 2,000 miles to the U.S. mainland.

Is the morale of "statesiders" here similar to teachers

on the mainland? How do Filipino teachers, who also came
here as strangers, compare in morale to U.S. mainlanders?
Are the stateside teachers as satisfied as the Filipinos?
How do these two groups compare in morale with the local
Chamorros? The assessment of morale and satisfaction in the
proposed study will attempt to answer these questions.

A number of U.S. studies conducted during the past
fifteen years indicate that the morale of teachers is
continuing on a downward slope. Fuller and Miskel (1972)
found that almost ninety percent of the teachers they
surveyed were satisfied or very satisfied with their jobs.
Eight years later, Bentzen, Williams, and Heckman (1980)
reported that slightly more than seventy-five percent of
the teachers in their study were satisfied with their
jobs. Thirty-five percent of all public school teachers
noted dissatisfaction with their current employment in a
nation-wide poll of teachers conducted by the National
Education Association (NEA) in 1980. Additionally, two out
of every five teachers said that if given the chance to
start their careers over again, they would probably do
something else rather than go into teaching. Ten percent
of the teachers said they were going to depart the
profession and another twenty percent said they did not
know how long they would continue teaching.

Measures of Teacher Morale and Satisfaction. Various
assessment instruments have been devised to measure teacher
morale. The School Organization Development Questionnaire,
developed by Mullen (1974), has a section that assesses
teacher morale. The School Climate Profile, developed by
Shaheen and Pedrick (1974), focuses on teacher
satisfaction. The Inventory of Leaders' Potential for
Facilitating Staff Morale, recently developed by Andrew,
Parks, and Nelson (1984), measures ten variables that make
up morale. Bentley and Rempel (1980) developed the Purdue
Teacher Opinionaire as a measure of teacher satisfaction
and morale. The Purdue Teacher Opinionaire yields a total
score that indicates the teacher's overall level of morale,
and subscores that indicate level of satisfaction with ten
work conditions: (1) teacher rapport with principal, (2)
satisfaction with teaching, (3) rapport among teachers, (4)
teacher salary, (5) teacher load, (6) curriculum issues,
(7) teacher status, (8) community support of education, (9)
school facilities and services, and (10) community
pressures. The Purdue Teacher Opinionaire has been chosen
as the assessment instrument for this study because it is a
widely used measure of teacher morale and satisfaction.

The demographic questionnaire sheet in the study will
contain a global question, "Generally, what is your morale
level?" Teachers will respond to this question on a
seven-point scale. This question differs from the Purdue
Teacher Opinionaire (PTO) in that it allows teachers to

give a personal estimate of their level of morale, whereas the PTO assesses satisfaction with ten working conditions, with the total score indicating the level of a teacher's morale. In other words, the PTO does not make a clear distinction between morale and satisfaction. The proposed study will use the PTO to measure satisfaction and the seven-point single-item scale to measure morale.

Significance of the Study

This investigation was stimulated by my participation in the development of the Blueprint for Excellence (Guam Department of Education, 1986). This report raised questions about the relationship between pupil achievement, teacher performance, and various job site conditions.

The Blueprint argued that "teachers are the single most important instructional variable and as such must be given maximum support..." The authors recommended that the Department create opportunities for teachers' professional growth and development, and incentives and recognition for exceptional performance, including sabbatical leave for all employees. The authors implied that a relationship exists between satisfaction and performance.

The success or failure of our public school system may depend on the degree to which educational administrators understand and focus on factors that satisfy or dissatisfy teachers as they plan and implement staff development programs. In a study of this problem, Quitugua (1975) used a sample of Guam public school teachers with a focus on "off-island contract teachers." He investigated factors that affected teacher satisfaction and tenure in the Guam public schools. The primary focus was to identify reasons for stateside teachers leaving or staying in the system. He did not draw any conclusions regarding the overall morale level of teachers in general in the Guam public school system.

A study of factors affecting teacher satisfaction using a nationally normed assessment instrument has not been conducted locally. As a result, educators can not determine if the teaching population of Guam is similar to staffs of mainland school districts. The proposed study will use a nationally normed instrument which will allow comparisons between Guam teachers and teachers in other school districts. If the findings reveal that the Guam teaching force is similar to staffs of mainland school districts, similar techniques for coping with low morale or trying to improve conditions to raise teacher satisfaction should apply here. If, however, Guam teachers are found to be significantly different from stateside teachers, Guam education officials will need to determine how to effectively cope with low morale or dissatisfying job site conditions locally.

The results of this study will identify the factors that possibly influence satisfaction or dissatisfaction of Guam teachers. Such information should allow administrators in the Department of Education to make more informed decisions regarding recruitment of teachers, preservice training of teachers, inservice training of teachers, and staff development of teachers and administrators.

If this study finds that teachers within a particular age group are more satisfied than others, the Department of Education should focus recruiting efforts on the more desirable age group. If the survey identified specific worksite characteristics which are more satisfying, then the Department should focus on equitably providing such conditions at all schools.

Communicating the findings to the Territorial Board of Education, the Guam Legislature, and the Executive Branch should enable these decision-makers to make more informed choices regarding decisions which impact upon teacher job site conditions that affect morale.

Decision-makers on the Board of Education, in the Executive Branch of Government, and in the Legislature should be informed as to those conditions that satisfy or dissatisfy teachers so they can make better informed decisions. If teachers are satisfied with intrinsic factors more than extrinsic ones, decision-makers should focus on those factors that satisfy and try to eliminate those that dissatisfy teachers.

Research Questions

The research questions to be answered by this study are as follows:

1. What is the current level of teacher satisfaction and morale on Guam?

2. What aspects of working conditions do teachers find satisfying or dissatisfying?

3. Is teacher morale related to satisfaction with particular worksite conditions?

4. Is teacher satisfaction related to ethnicity, gender, age, college training, teaching assignment, and length of teaching service?

REVIEW OF THE LITERATURE

The review of literature will follow the outline and cover the same topics as are found in the background section in Chapter 1. The review of literature will be in greater depth and will be presented in three parts. Part I will discuss research and theory on the construct of employee morale and satisfaction, particularly as it relates to teachers. Part II will review research on the effects of teacher morale and satisfaction on their productivity. Part III will review research on the factors that influence morale and satisfaction.

METHOD

The proposed study employs descriptive and
correlational research designs. The correlational part of
the study will involve correlating each of the dependent
variables (satisfaction and morale) with each of the
independent variables (ethnicity, sex, age, college
training, teaching assignment, and years of teaching
experience). The descriptive part of the study will
involve characterizing the sample on the various measures
of satisfaction and morale.

Subjects

Three hundred fourteen of the 1,256 (exactly 25
percent) teachers in grades kindergarten through twelve in
Guam public schools will be involved in the study. Only
full-time certified classroom teachers will be surveyed.
Teachers eliminated from the population include the
following: unqualified teachers, guidance counselors,
school health counselors, special education teachers,
teachers paid by the elementary division, teachers paid by
the secondary division, PACE (Planned Alternative Center
for Education) teachers, LAMP (Language Arts and Math
Program) teachers, GATE (Gifted and Talented Education)
HEAD START teachers, Chamorro Studies teachers, and
Bilingual/Bicultural teachers.

Stratified sampling by school of the regular classroom
teachers was accomplished using a systematic sampling
procedure outlined in Borg and Gall (1983) for regular,
certified classroom teachers listed by the Office of
Research, Planning, and Evaluation.

Teachers' names were provided in random order by
school. Starting with the eighth number, determined by
throwing two dice, every fourth person in the 1,256-person
listing was chosen. When the final person at the end of
the list was selected, the process proceeded by continuing
the selection process at the beginning of the list, up to
the eighth name.

An identification number known only to the author was
included on each questionnaire. All participants were
notified of their selection. A letter explaining the study
and plans to protect the identity of each participant was
distributed. The letter is shown in Appendix A. (Appendix
A is not included here. Interested readers can find
material presented in it in the completed dissertation.

Measures

Demographic Information. A questionnaire to collect demographic information about each teacher in the sample was developed. Respondents will be asked to indicate personal information regarding: ethnicity (Chamorro, Caucasian, Filipino, other); gender (female, male); age (29 or under, 30-39, 40-49, 50 or over); years of college training (less than a B.A.; B.A. or B.S.; Master's degree; Master's degree plus 30 hours; Specialist degree; or Ph.D/Ed.D.); current level of teaching assignment (elementary, middle school, high school); and years of experience, including this year, teaching in any school district (1 year, 2-4 years, 5-9 years, and 10 years and over). This instrument is shown in Appendix B. (Appendix B is not included here. Interested readers can find material presented in it in the completed dissertation.)

Teacher Morale. This variable will be measured by a single item. Teachers will be asked to estimate their level of morale by circling a number on a seven-point scale.

Teacher Satisfaction. The Purdue Teacher Opinionaire (PTO), Revised Form, will be used to provide a measure of teacher satisfaction. The Purdue Teacher Opinionaire yields a total score indicating teachers' overall level of satisfaction, and a subscore for level of satisfaction with each of the following work conditions:

1. Teacher rapport with principal -- deals with the teacher's feelings about the principal and his/her professional competency, interest in teachers and their work, ability to communicate, and skill in human relations.

2. Satisfaction with teaching -- pertains to the teacher's relationships with students and feelings of satisfaction with teaching.

3. Rapport among teachers -- focuses on the teacher's relationships with other teachers. The items solicit the teacher's opinion regarding the cooperation, preparation, ethics influence, interests, and competency of the teacher's peers.

4. Teacher salary -- pertains primarily to the teacher's feelings about salaries and salary policies.

5. Teacher load -- deals with such matters as record-keeping, clerical work, "red tape," community demands on teacher time, extra-curricular load, and keeping up-to-date professionally.

6. _Curriculum issues_ -- solicits teacher reactions to adequacy of the school program in meeting student needs, in providing for individual differences, and in preparing students for effective citizenship.

7. _Teacher status_ -- samples feelings about the prestige, security, and benefits afforded by teaching. Several of the items refer to the extent to which the teacher feels accepted by the community.

8. _Community support of education_ -- deals with the extent to which the community understands and is willing to support a sound educational program.

9. _School facilities and services_ -- has to do with the adequacy of facilities, supplies, and equipment, and the efficiency of the procedures for obtaining materials and services.

10. _Community pressures_ -- concerns community expectations with respect to the teacher's personal standards, participation in outside school activities, and freedom to discuss controversial issues in the classroom.

In a critique quoted in _The Seventh Mental Measurements Yearbook_ (Buros, 1978), Benjamin Rosner stated that the PTO "appears to be a carefully constructed research instrument." It can give an estimate of individual teacher, school, or system-wide morale. The _Yearbook_ reported that the reliability of the total score on the instrument was .87. The reliability of the individual scales ranges from .62 (community pressures) to .88 (teacher rapport with principal). The median reliability coefficient for the ten factor scores is .80. The _Yearbook_ concluded that, "in general, the data suggest that the relative stability of both the total and separate factor scores -- with the exception of the community pressures factors -- is clearly adequate for research purposes and equally adequate for large group assessment."

The _Manual for the Purdue Teacher Opinionaire_ stated that there is "no relevant criterion on which to judge the validity of an instrument of this nature, except, to some extent, the performance of teachers." Bentley and Rempel, authors of the instrument, wrote, "To the extent that teachers agree with one another, are self consistent in their ratings, and content validity is exhibited, at least adequate validity may be assumed."

Data Collection

The author will meet with the principals of the thirty-five participating schools during regularly scheduled principals' meetings to solicit support and explain the study. Following a briefing, principals will be asked to handcarry questionnaires to their school. They will be asked to request their secretary to collect the completed questionnaires in sealed envelopes, as they are returned by the teachers. The sealed questionnaires are to be placed in a manila envelope, which will be picked up by the author.

Approval for the study was granted by the district, through the Department of Education's "Educational Research Review Panel."

The Purdue Teacher Opinionaire, demographic questionnaire, and cover letter will be distributed to all Department of Education classroom teachers on or about March 1, 1987, with a requested return date of one week later.

Teachers will be informed that all information will be kept CONFIDENTIAL in the preliminary notification letter, in the instructions, and on the questionnaire form. Also, they will be informed that they should make no identifying marks on the questionnaire or on the envelope that is to be returned to the researcher. Teachers will be informed that all data sheets will be destroyed following data entry into the computer. The author will have the only copy of identification numbers to be used in recording who responded to the questionnaires. Once information has been processed, questionnaires will be destroyed.

Permission to assess the public school teachers has been received from the Guam Department of Education's Research Review Committee.

The cooperation and assistance of elementary, middle, and high school principals will be solicited during briefings to be conducted at scheduled principals' meetings.

Data Analysis

Question one, "What is the current level of teacher morale on Guam?" will be analyzed using descriptive statistics.

Question two, "What aspects of working conditions do teachers find satisfying or dissatisfying?" will be analyzed using descriptive statistics.

Question three, "What aspects of working conditions affect teacher morale?" will be analyzed using correlational statistics.

Question four, "Are teacher satisfaction and morale related to the factors of ethnicity, sex, age, college training, teaching assignment, and years of experience?" will be analyzed using correlational statistics.

Trained computer analysts from the Office of Research, Planning, and Evaluation, will enter data during off-time hours. Responses of each participating teacher will be entered by one analyst and another analyst will verify the accuracy of each entry.

Project Timeline

1. March 3
   Begin distribution of Teacher Questionnaires to public   schools

2. March 12 - 13
   Begin collecting completed Questionnaires at all public schools sites. Distribute reminder notes to all teachers who have not completed and turned in Questionnaire.

3. March 16
   Begin entering information into computer memory for data analysis.

4. March 18
   Contact principals and request that they remind teachers about completing Questionnaire

5. March 20
   Initiate telephone contact procedures to request that teachers complete and return Questionnaire.
   Continue entering data.

6. March 25
   Begin data analysis
   a. Double-check data entries against codebook.
   b. Frequency distributions on all variables to identify "outliers".

7. April 1
   Initiate dissertation data analysis.
   Begin working on "write-ups," charts, and chapter IV.

BIBLIOGRAPHY

Bentley, R.R., and Rempel, A.M. Manual for the Purdue
   Teacher Opinionaire. 2nd rev. ed. West Lafayette,
   Ind.: Purdue Research Foundation, 1980.

Bentley, R.R. "Peer-selection vs. expert judgment as a
   means of validating a teacher morale measuring
   instrument." Journal of Experimental Education, 1963,
   31, 235-45.

Berry, B. "Why Miss Dove left and where she went: A case
   study of teacher attrition in a metropolitan school
   system in the southwest." Occasional paper in education
   policy analysis. Paper No. 414. Washington, D.C.:
   National Institute of Education, 1985 (ED 256 071 ERIC)

Cruz-Rodriguez, A. "The application of Herzberg's theory
   of motivation to work to public elementary school
   teachers in Puerto Rico." Dissertation Abstracts
   International, 1980, 41., 2369A. (University
   Microfilms No. 8027436).

Engleking, J.L. "Identification of satisfying and
   dissatisfying factors in staffs of elementary and
   secondary public school teachers from two states." 1985

Freese, A.J. The relationship between school morale and
   the congruency of perceptions of high school principals
   and teachers concerning selected leadership styles.)
   Doctoral dissertation, Ohio University, 1984).
   Dissertation Abstracts International, 45 2328A.

Hansford, B., "Personal and Professional Problems,"
   Guidebook for School Principals, 1961, pp. 26-27.

Holdway, E.A. "Facet and overall satisfaction of
   teachers." Educational Administration Quarterly, 1978,
   14(1), 30-47.

Jaycox, W., and Tallman, L. "A study of the motivation of
   elementary school teachers. "Dissertation Abstracts
   International, 28, 81A. (University Microfilms No.
   67-8033)

Lebovitz, G. "Satisfaction and dissatisfaction among
   Judaic Studies teachers in Midwestern Jewish day
   schools." Dissertation Abstracts International, 1981,
   43. 35A (University Microfilms No. 820-7120)

Medved, J.A. "The applicability of Herzberg's
   motivational-hygiene theory. Educational Leadership,
   1989, 39, 555.

Miller, W.C., "Staff Morale, School Climate and Educational Productivity," <u>Educational Leadership</u>, 1981, p. 483

Miles, M.P. "A comparative study of teacher morale in districts experiencing varying enrollment trends." (Doctoral dissertation, Temple University, (1985) <u>Dissertation Abstracts International</u>, 46 2153A.

Murphy, M.L. An analysis of teacher incentives and disincentives relative to teacher retention. (Doctoral dissertation, University of Nevada, 1985. <u>Dissertation Abstracts International</u> 46, 2149A.

National Education Association. <u>Project: Time to Teach</u>. Washington, D.C.: Department of Classroom Teachers, 1966.

Ramsey, R.d., <u>Management Techniques for Solving School Personnel Problems,</u> West Nyack, N.Y.: Parker Publishing, 1984.

Smith, K.R. "A Proposed Model for the Investigation of Teacher Morale." <u>Journal of Educational Administration</u>, 1966. 4, 143-48.

Stanley, G., and Hansen, O. " Study of the Motivation of high school teachers." <u>Dissertation Abstracts International</u>, 1969, 30. 4148A. (University Microfilms No. 70-5209).

Watson, G. "Five Factors in Morale." In <u>Civilian Morale,</u> edited by G. Watson. Boston: Houghton Mifflin, 1942.

Sandra M. Simons

<u>Dissertation Proposal</u>

The Effects of Training Secondary Teachers in a Reading
Comprehension Instruction Strategy Based on Schema
Theory

Information about the completed dissertation is in
<u>Dissertation Abstracts International</u>, vol. 45, no. 7,
section A, page 2052.
The DAI order number is DER 84-22871.

INTRODUCTION

Purpose

The purpose of this study is to develop and test an instructional strategy to improve secondary readers' comprehension of expository text. The investigation will determine to what extent teachers implement the strategy after inservice training and whether the strategy facilitates students' comprehension of expository text.

Background

Recent empirical studies show that "time-on-task" or "pupil engaged time" is an important variable in reading achievement (Stallings and Kaskowitz, 1974; Evertson, Anderson and Brophy, 1978; Rosenshine, 1979). Just as important as spending time on reading, however, is how that time is spent. Several researchers (Stallings, 1980; Anderson, Evertson and Brophy, 1979; Crawford et al., 1978) have identified teaching practices related to improved reading achievement. Jane Stallings identified specific teaching practices that produce a gain in reading achievement of secondary readers. She found that the most effective teachers are engaged 50 percent of the reading instructional time period in "interactive" instruction which includes; discussing and reviewing; drill and practice; corrective feedback; and instruction.

In an experimental study, Stallings (1982) successfully trained teachers to meet her criteria for effective use of time. Students of the trained teachers showed higher achievement gains than students of teachers who did not use their time as effectively.

In my recent conversations with Jane Stallings, she identified the need to provide teachers with techniques for teaching comprehension. She explained that she is able to train teachers to organize and manage their time effectively and to provide interactive instruction. Her observations reveal, however, that during the time she designates as interactive instruction, little instruction in comprehension occurs.

Stallings's observation that comprehension instruction in classrooms is lacking is supported by recent descriptive studies that indicate that most reading instruction does not include instruction in comprehension. Duffy and

McIntyre (1980) observed six primary grade teachers during reading instruction. They found that teachers monitored students through commercial materials and that the major instructional activity was to assess the accuracy of student responses. Follow-up interviews with teachers indicated that they perceived their job as guiding students through materials.

Other studies of classroom practices show that most teacher-pupil interaction during reading instruction is one in which the teacher asks a question and the student responds. Occasionally, the teacher provides an evaluative response (Dunkin and Biddle, 1974; Mehan, 1979).

Dolores Durkin (1978-1979) analyzed 7,244 minutes of observation of reading instruction in 24 fourth-grade classrooms in 13 different school systems. She found that teachers spent less that one percent of the reading instructional time (28 minutes) on comprehension instruction. She defined comprehension instruction as the "teacher does/says something to help children understand or work out the meaning of more than a single isolated word" (p.488). Durkin found that what teachers spent their time on was assessment of comprehension with literal questions from manuals (17%); assignment-giving, monitoring, and checking (14%); transition activities (10%) and noninstructional activities such as grading papers at their desks (19%).

In the same study Durkin also looked at reading instruction in 12 other classrooms, grades three through six. She found that no comprehension instruction occurred. The main concern of teachers was to see that students completed assignments with correct answers. She concluded that teachers do not provide comprehension instruction but instead are "assignment-givers" who rely heavily on the use of workbooks and dittos.

Edith Slinger (1981) observed 59.1 hours of instruction in content classrooms of four secondary schools. She found that only six percent of classroom time was devoted to reading instruction. Furthermore, one of the four schools accounted for one-half of the total observed time in reading instruction.

The observations of Stallings, Durkin, and others suggested the proposed study. Jane Stallings invited me to join her in developing methods for comprehension instruction that could be taught to teachers in the fifth workshop of her inservice program called "Effective Use of Time Training." In this fifth workshop, entitled "Improving Instruction and Monitoring," Stallings presents ideas for teaching reading.

A review of the literature revealed little empirical research on instructional techniques for improving the reading comprehension of secondary students. In a recent review of research on instructional strategies for improving the comprehension of adolescent readers, Joseph Vaughan (1981) concluded that "research in reading in secondary schools is sparse at best" (p.16). He also observed that the instructional strategies advocated do not work. Others have been tested with elementary or college students and then advocated for use with secondary students.

Because of the lack of empirically validated instructional comprehension strategies for use with secondary remedial readers, I decided to develop a research-based strategy to improve the reading comprehension of this population of students.

A review of the literature suggested that schema theory and research provide a promising base for developing an instructional strategy to teach reading comprehension. Schema theorists believe that schemata are conceptual mental frameworks that facilitate readers' comprehension of ideas in text. Two types of schemata enable readers to integrate new information into their memory: content schemata, which are what the reader already knows about a topic; and textual schemata, which are frameworks for understanding and using different text organization (Anderson, Pichert and Shirey, 1979). Empirical research has demonstrated that readers with well-developed schemata have better comprehension of ideas in text than readers with weaker schemata.

The comprehension instruction strategy to be developed and tested in the proposed study is intended to accomplish two purposes. First, the strategy is intended to activate and organize the student's content schema, that is, their existing knowledge. The second purpose is to develop students' textual schema, that is, to teach students to use text organization to understand what they read. Jane Stallings's inservice program "Effective Use of Time Training" will provide a setting in which teachers can be trained in the comprehension instruction strategy and in which implementation and student effects can be assessed.

Significance

The major benefit of the proposed study is that it will contribute to knowledge about how to teach reading comprehension. Also, the study will test the applicability of schema theory to problems of reading instruction.

The study should be of particular interest to preservice and inservice teacher educators. Durkin (1981) suggested that the lack of reading comprehension instruction in classrooms is caused by the failure of manuals to provide teaching suggestions. Another cause of this instructional deficit, however, may be that teachers are inadequately trained in methods that both work and are possible to implement. If the proposed study demonstrates that teachers can be trained to implement the strategy, teacher educators may be encouraged to include it in their preservice and inservice programs.

Research Objectives

The objectives of this study are:

1.   To develop an instructional strategy to improve secondary readers' comprehension of expository text.

2.   To determine the extent to which teachers implement the strategy after training.

3.   To determine whether teachers' use of the strategy facilitates secondary readers' comprehension of expository text.

REVIEW OF THE LITERATURE

Four lines of research are relevant to this study:
research on current practices in teaching reading
comprehension: research on the theoretical foundations of
the comprehension strategy; research on effective teaching
practices; and research on effective procedures in
inservice training.

Research on Current Practices in

Teaching Reading Comprehension

Descriptive studies by Durkin (1979-80), Slinger (1981)
and others indicate that little or no instruction in
comprehension occurs during the reading instructional time
or during content area instruction. These studies were
described in Part I. This lack of reading comprehension
instruction has several explanations. Durkin (1981)
attributes the problem to a lack of teaching suggestions in
teaching manuals. In her content analysis of teaching
manuals for five basal reading series, Durkin found that
most suggestions involved assessing comprehension, not
teaching it.
Some authorities attribute the lack of comprehension
instruction to the fact that teachers are not adequately
trained to teach reading comprehension, especially at the
secondary level (Cramer, 1978). Many states have no
requirement for secondary teachers to take a methods course
in teaching reading and study skills. Many reading
teachers in the secondary schools have had no formal
training in reading instruction.
Vaughan (1981) thinks that the lack of reading
instruction at the secondary level is due to the paucity of
empirically validated strategies for use with secondary
readers. Many of the widely advocated strategies have
never been empirically validated with secondary students,
and many do not work (Vaughan, 1981; Graves and Clark,
1981). For example, the Directed Reading-Thinking Activity
(DR-TA) is intended to improve students' comprehension and
is recommended in most secondary reading textbooks. It has
only been tested, however, with _elementary_ students. SQ3R,
a reading-study strategy, has been advocated for over two
decades, but lacks rigorous empirical validation. Of the
few studies that have been done, none support its use.

Another factor that contributes to the problem is that many recommended strategies are difficult to implement. In their investigations of SQ3R, Willmore (1967) and Wooster (1959) both concluded that this method was too difficult to teach and that other strategies such as reading and underlining are more effective and efficient. Initial investigations of the Construct Procedure (Vaughan, 1981), a strategy for teaching students how to understand expository text, have had positive results. Vaughan reports, however, that the strategy is complex and that it takes a minimum of two class periods during each of ten consecutive weeks to train students to successfully use the strategy. Vaughan did not consider whether teachers would be willing to attempt to implement such a complex strategy.

The instructional strategy developed in this study was designed to both improve student reading comprehension and to be easily implemented by teachers. The study will investigate whether teachers can implement the strategy after four to five hours of inservice training and whether the strategy is effective in facilitating comprehension.

Table 1. Reading Comprehension Strategy

Summary

STEP I: FIND OUT WHAT STUDENTS ALREADY KNOW

   *1.   Read the selection. Pick out key concepts, vocabulary, and main ideas.
    2.   Ask questions and probes to find out what students already know about the key concepts, vocabulary, and main ideas in the selection.
    3.   Provide background information as necessary.

STEP II: HELP STUDENTS SEE HOW THE TEXT IS ORGANIZED

   *4.   Prepare an overview of the selection.
        Prepare a blank overview for the students
    5.   Distribute the blank overview to the students. Explain what the students will do with the overview.
    6.   Draw a blank overview on the chalkboard. Help students fill in part of the overview with chalkboard information that is included in the selection.

STEP III: HAVE STUDENTS READ THE SELECTION

    7.   Set the purpose for reading by telling the students to:
        - read to verify information they already know
        - read to find new information
        - think about how new information will fit into the overview.
    8.   Have students read the selection silently or aloud in small groups.
    9.   Have students complete the overview.

STEP IV: DISCUSS THE SELECTION

   10.   Complete the chalkboard overview by calling on specific students to provide information.
   11.   Ask questions that have students summarize the selection.
   12.   Ask questions that encourage students to think about the selection.

---

* Teacher completes before instruction.

<u>Theoretical Foundations of the</u>

<u>Comprehension Instruction Strategy</u>

The comprehension instruction strategy (see Table 1) is based on current cognitive theories of learning and the research that supports them. This section of the literature review discusses the theoretical underpinnings and supporting research for the strategy.

<u>Interactive Instruction.</u> Recent research indicates that successful reading comprehension instructional strategies are highly interactive. In a number of studies, Stallings (1979, 1980) identified several variables within the secondary classroom that correlate with improved reading achievement. The primary indicator of reading achievement is the teacher-pupil interaction. Students in classrooms where teachers guided and directed students' reading had higher achievement gains than classrooms where teachers did not interact as much with students. Little improvement was observed in classes where teachers did not interact with students. Vaughan (1981) reached a similar conclusion in his review of secondary reading instructional strategies. He concluded that of the instructional strategies that have been investigated, those that have a high level of teacher-student interaction are most successful.

The comprehension instruction strategy developed in this study is highly interactive. The teacher helps students to brainstorm associations to main concepts, structures the text for students, sets the purpose for reading, and asks questions about the selection content.

<u>Reader-Text Interaction.</u> The prevalent theoretical perspective on reading is that the reader is an active agent who directs an interchange with the text (Pearson and Kamil, 1980). Reading theorists view comprehension as an active process in which readers make hypotheses about text meaning as they read, and then test their hypotheses. If their hypotheses are confirmed or refuted, understanding occurs and they continue to read smoothly. If the text fails to make sense and a hypothesis cannot be confirmed or refuted, good readers take action to promote understanding (Singer and Rudell, 1976).

The comprehension instruction strategy developed in this study is designed to encourage the student to interact with the text. Activating prior knowledge purpose setting, and structuring the text are techniques in the strategy that encourage readers to make hypotheses about what they will read and to confirm or to refute them. Another technique, filling in an overview, helps readers see where understanding fails so that they can take remedial action to understand the text.

   Schema Theory: Content Schemata. Many reading researchers believe that background knowledge affects what is recalled from reading. Ausubel (1978), for example, stated:
>   If I had to reduce all of educational
>   psychology to one principle, I would say
>   this: The most important single factor
>   influencing learning is what the learner
>   already knows. Ascertain this and teach
>   him accordingly. (p.iv)

   Like Ausubel, schema theorists believe prior knowledge is essential to learning. They believe schemata are an important element in the comprehension of the text. Rumelhart and Ortony (1977) define schemata as abstract mental frameworks that incorporate a person's general knowledge. The reader's existing knowledge about a topic is his or her content schemata. Comprehension occurs when new information from text is linked to existing content schemata (Anderson, Pichert, and Shirey, 1979). Thelen (1976) compared a person's schemata or existing mental frameworks to a person's ideational filing system. Within that filing system are files or schemata for certain categories of information. Likening prior knowledge to new information involves finding the proper file in which to store new information.
   A number of empirical studies lend support to the theoretical construct of content schemata. Anderson, Reynolds, Shallert, and Goetz (1977) showed that readers make inferences consistent with their schemata. They presented college students from music and physical education classes with text passages that could have two interpretations. One passage could be interpreted as being about a convict planning an escape from prison or as about a wrestler trying to break the hold of an opponent. The second passage could be interpreted as a group of friends getting together to play cards or for a rehearsal session of an ensemble. A test of free recall of text and a multiple-choice test indicated that students gave each passage one interpretation or another based on their special interests. Students in the weightlifting class gave the first passage a wrestling interpretation; music students made the other interpretation. In reading the second passage, the music students made the rehearsal interpretation, and the P.E. students made the card-playing interpretation. Subjects reported that they

were unaware of the other interpretation as they read. The results of this study demonstrate that schemata provide an interpretive framework for comprehending text and that a person's schemata cause him or her to understand text in certain ways.

In an earlier study using ambiguous passages, Bransford and McCarrell (1974) reported similar results. They gave students a passage that could have either a peace march or spaceship landing interpretation. They found that subjects recalled information consistent with their background experiences.

Anderson, Spiro, and Anderson (1978) demonstrated that readers recall text information important to their schema. A total of 75 college students, all of whom had a well-defined schema for fine restaurants, read one of two narratives. One narrative was about a meal in a restaurant; the other about a trip to the supermarket. The passages contained the same target information: eighteen food items mentioned in the same order. The order followed categories of food served in a fine restaurant: appetizers, entree, and dessert. On a test of free recall of text, subjects who read the restaurant passages had superior recall of foods determined to be a part of a person's fine-restaurant schema than subjects who read the supermarket passage. This experiment provides support for the theory that information that is incorporated into a existing schema is better learned and recalled than information that cannot be linked to an existing schema.

Pearson (1979) investigated whether the background experiences that a reader brings to a selection affects his or her depth of understanding. Pearson's study differed from previous ones in four ways: (a) he used unambiguous text rather than ambiguous text, (b) be used second graders rather than college students, (c) he used wh- questions for the test rather than free recall, and (d) he manipulated prior knowledge by assessing what students already knew about the text rather than by implementing schematic information in the readers' minds or in the passage. Pearson found that students with a great amount of prior knowledge about the text content (in this case, spiders) answered more wh- questions correctly than those with little prior knowledge. His results confirm and extend the conclusions of schema theorists about the effect of schemata on comprehension: readers with well-developed schemata about a topic are able to answer more questions about a passage than those with weakly developed schemata.

The proposed comprehension strategy is intended to activate the reader's schema to help him or her link new information from text with existing knowledge. If the teacher finds that students do not have adequately developed schemata for the reading, he or she should provide needed background information. The strategy also helps students see how new information links with what they already know by organizing the readers' prior knowledge with a visual overview before reading and by having students complete the overview with new information after reading.

    Schema Theory: Textual Schemata. Schema theorists believe that the reader not only has content schemata but also textual schemata, that is, knowledge of text organization. Knowledge about types of text forms and how those forms are organized is thought to affect the reader's ability to learn from text (Anderson, Pichert, and Shirey, 1979). The majority of expository text are organized by superordinate or main ideas. Subordinate ideas explain and describe the superordinate ideas. In contrast, fiction is organized by presenting a problem, building action to a climax, and concluding with a resolution. Schema theory posits that good readers have schemata for these various text organizations and use them to remember what they read.

    Empirical studies suggest that an awareness of the organization and relationships among concepts in expository texts facilitates understanding and recall. Meyers (1975) found that good readers tend to recall generalizations better than specifics. Meyer, Brandt, and Bluth (1980) found that good readers used the same structures as the author for organizing information to be recalled.

    Vacca (1975) conducted an experiment in seventh-grade social studies classes to test the effects of pattern guides on reading comprehension. A pattern guide (Vacca, 1981) is a reading-study aid made up of questions that help the reader recognize and use the author's organization. Results of the experiment showed that pattern guides aid students in recognizing organizational patterns in expository text and improve their learning of content ideas.

    Mapping, or diagramming text organization, has been shown to be an effective aid to comprehension. Holliday and Harvey (1976) found that subjects who read and used diagrams of the text material scored higher on a multiple-choice posttest than did subjects who only read the text. Ambruster and Anderson (1980) investigated the effectiveness of mapping on the comprehension of middle school students. In mapping, students identify text structure and diagram-related ideas. They trained one group of eighth graders to map expository passages. To test the strategy, they gave the trained and untrained students two expository passages to read. Trained students who mapped the two passages recalled a greater proportion of idea units than those who used their own reading strategy. The researchers concluded that mapping may be an effective aid for recalling some types of expository text.

Some research has been done on networking, a strategy similar to mapping in that students graphically represent relationships in text. Dansereau (1979) found that networking aids reading comprehension in adults. No studies to date have been done with secondary students.

Metacognitive researchers have also studied the relationship of text structure to reading for understanding. An assumption of metacognitive theory is that effective learners are aware of text structure and use that structure to help them remember information. The results of studies by Bransford, Stein, Shelton, and Owings (1980) showed differences between good and poor students in metacognitive knowledge of how to recognize text structure and to use it for remembering. In one study, the researchers presented fifth-grade students with passages of two types: (1) precise and logically structured, or (2) imprecise. The imprecise passages contained character descriptions that were incongruent with character behaviors. Students studied passages and then were tested for memory. Better students reported that imprecise passages were more difficult and that they spent more time studying them than the precise ones. Poorer students showed no awareness of differing text structure and no differences in study times across the two types of passages. In a later study, the same researchers found that poorer students, with training, could learn to spend differential study time on the two passage types.

The comprehension instruction strategy to be tested in the present study uses a graphic overview to develop students' textual schemata. The visual representation of the text organization is intended to help students recognize and use the author's organization to better understand the text.

Summary

The comprehension instruction strategy is based on current theory and research in the following ways:

1. Each step of the strategy encourages interactive instruction. Teachers ask questions, lead a discussion, and provide instruction.

2. The strategy activities encourage the reader to interact with the text.

3. In Step I, the teacher assesses and activates the reader's prior knowledge and provides needed background information.

4. In Steps II and IV, the teacher explains the text organization to students. The graphic overview helps students recognize and use the text organization to understand what they read. It also provides a way for students to link new information to what they already know.

Research on Effective Teaching Practices

Research on teaching effectiveness in the last decade has found that teacher practices do affect students' achievement in reading. Students whose teachers have organized, well-managed classrooms tend to have higher reading achievement scores than students of teachers whose instructional management is weak.

An important principle of instructional management is to use techniques that maximize students' time on task (also called "pupil engaged time"). Process-product studies have demonstrated that time on task correlates positively with reading achievement gains (Stallings and Kaskowitz, 1974; Evertson, Anderson, and Brophy, 1978; and Rosenshine, 1979). In an experiment involving students in third, fifth, and sixth grades who read below grade level, Wyne and Stuck (1979) found that students who were in an experimental treatment designed to increase "time on task" achieved higher reading sores than their counterparts in control classrooms.

Spending time on reading is important, but just as important is how that time is spent. Several researchers have used the finding of process-product studies to develop and experimentally test reading instruction strategies. Anderson, Evertson, and Brophy (1979 identified twenty-two principles for effective reading instruction in the first grade. The more general set of six principles is as follows:

1. Reading groups should be organized for efficient, sustained focus on the content to be learned.

2. All students should be... actively involved in the lesson.

3. The difficulty level of questions and tasks should be easy enough to enable the teacher to move the lesson along at a brisk pace and the students to experience consistent success.

4. Students should receive frequent opportunities to read and respond to questions and should get clear feedback about the correctness of their performance.

5. Skills should be mastered to overlearning, with new ones gradually phased in while old ones are being mastered.

6. Although instruction should take place in the group setting for efficiency reasons, the teacher monitors the progress of each individual student and provides specific instruction, feedback and practice as needed. (Anderson, et al, 1981)

The researchers taught the twenty-two principles to an experimental group of 27 first-grade teachers. The students of experimental teachers outperformed the students of an untrained group of teachers on reading achievement tests.

In a two-phase study of 87 secondary remedial reading classrooms, Stallings (1980) first conducted correlational research to identify effective teaching behaviors that produced a gain in reading scores for remedial secondary students. She found that the following interactive on-task behaviors were associated with improved reading achievement:

1. instructing and informing

2. discussing and reviewing written work and selection content

3. having students read aloud

4. providing praise and support

5. providing corrective feedback

6. questioning and checking for understanding.

Stallings found that effective teachers spend at least 50 percent of their time engaged in interactive instruction.

Stallings (1980) also identified less effective practices in which the student appeared to be on task but the teacher was not teaching. Those practices, called non-interactive on-task behaviors, included:

1. engaging in non-student tasks such as paper grading

2. monitoring silent reading

3. monitoring written seatwork

Stallings found that several off-task activities (transition time, social interactions, and disciplinary time) correlated negatively with reading achievement.

Table 2. How Effective Teachers Allocate Their Time

Organization/Management Activities	(15%)

     (E) Take roll
     (E) Make announcements
     (E) Make expectations clear for the period:
         quality and quantity of work
     (E) Clarify any behavior expectations
     (E) Pass papers or books (out and in)

Interactive On-Task Instruction	(50%)

     (E) Review/discuss previous work
     (E) Inform/instruct new concept
         (Demonstrate/give examples)
     (E) Question/check for understanding
     (S) Reteach small group (if necessary)
     (S) Read aloud/develop concepts
     (E) Summarize

Non-Interactive Instruction (Seatwork)	(35%)

     (L) Written work
     (L) Silent reading
     (L) Teacher monitoring/guiding

E = Total Class
S = Small Group
L = Large Group
I = Individual

The proposed comprehension instruction strategy will be investigated in the context of the model of effective teaching practices developed by Stallings (1982). The model is shown in summary form in Table 2. Stallings has not specifically identified the most effective content for instruction within her model of interactive on-task teaching. The comprehension instruction strategy will be that content. Training of teachers in the strategy will occur as a component of Stallings's inservice program on effective use of time.

Research on Effective Inservice Training

Teachers must receive effective inservice training if they are to implement new techniques successfully. Four recent experiments have suggested some elements of effective inservice training. All four experiments compared teaching practices of an untrained group of teachers and a trained group of teachers as well as the achievement gains of their students. In each case the trained teachers implemented the desired practices more than did the untrained teachers. Also, student achievement gains of the trained teachers were greater than those of the untrained teachers.

In one of the experiments, Crawford and colleagues (1978) assigned 33 third-grade teachers to a control group or one of two treatment groups: a maximum training group and a minimum training group. The maximally trained teachers attended five weekly workshops and received a packet of training materials. The minimally trained teachers received only the training packets. Both the maximally and minimally trained teachers implemented, on the average, more of the suggested practices than did the control group teachers. Not all trained teachers implemented practices to the same degree, however. The students of both groups of trained teachers gained significantly more in reading than did students of the control group teachers. There was no difference between the two treatment group teachers in their average use of the recommended practices.

Interview data suggested that two practices that were very specific were implemented to a high degree. More global, abstract, and complex recommendations were less successfully implemented. Teachers also mentioned that implementation of practices was influenced by the compatibility of the practices with their philosophy.

Anderson, Evertson, and Brophy (1979) conducted an experiment with 27 first-grade teachers. The researchers met twice with the 17 experimental-group teachers and gave them a manual describing the training model. Their results

were similar to those of Crawford and colleagues (1978).
The trained teachers implemented the recommendations more
than did the untrained teachers. Not all teachers
implemented all recommendations to the same degree. Those
practices that were implemented were specific and made
sense to teachers. The researchers concluded that teachers
may not implement practices that are novel, complex, or
demand extra time and energy unless they are given both
specific assistance in implementation and are convinced of
the usefulness of the practice.

Good and Grouws (1979) trained twenty fourth-grade math
teachers in two 90-minute training sessions. Experimental
group teachers also received a manual with instructional
suggestions. Good and Grouws found that teachers
implemented the more specific recommendations. The
teachers who had the highest degree of implementation were
those who found the practices congruent with their values
and teaching styles.

Stallings, Needels, and Strayrook (1979) conducted an
experiment involving secondary remedial reading teachers.
They began by observing the 25 experimental group teachers
before training. They used the data to create an
individual teaching profile for each teacher. The profile
indicated the teacher's current practices and compared them
to a criterion established in previous studies for
effective use of time in secondary remedial reading
classrooms. The 25 teachers then attended six 2 1/2 hour,
small-group training sessions. Stallings and her
colleagues used an interactive, group problem-solving
approach to training. They encouraged teachers to share
ideas and problems. After training, teachers were again
observed for three full class sessions.

Results indicated that the trained teachers improved
their performance on most but not all of the
recommendations. Similar results were obtained in a second
study. The two practices that teachers tended not to
implement in either study were reading aloud and grouping.
The researchers explained that these ideas are not
congruent with secondary teachers' style or training. The
researchers concluded that "teachers can and do make
changes in organization and management style when changes
are practical and can be adapted to their own environment"
(pp.13-15).

Mohlman, Coladarci, and Gage (1982) suggested that the
high degree of implementation achieved in the Stallings
experiment was due to the interactive, supportive
atmosphere of the training sessions. Philosophical
objections and difficulties in classroom application of
practices could be worked out in this training climate.
Also, the extensive training may have made it possible for
some teachers to successfully implement complex and novel

practices.

These experiments indicate that the effectiveness of inservice training depends on presenting recommendations specifically and clearly. Furthermore, implementation of more complex practices requires extensive, supportive training with encouragement of interaction between teachers.

Stallings's model of training will be used to train teachers in the use of the proposed comprehension instruction strategy. Training in the strategy will include two workshops, each 2 1/2 hours, that will be integrated into Stallings's inservice program "Effective Use of Time Training." A detailed description of this program is presented in the next part of this proposal (see Table 4).

METHOD

Research Design

The proposed experiment will follow a nonequivalent control group design. The design is graphically represented as follows:

E_1	$O_{1,2,3}$	X_1	$O_{4,5,6}$
E_2	$O_{1,2,3}$	X_2	$O_{4,5,6}$
E_3			O_4

Where E_1 =   Group of teachers who receive maximum training

E_2 =   Group of teachers who receive minimal training

E_3 =   Group of teachers who receive no training

$O_{1,2,3}$ = Baseline measures of teacher and student performance

X_1 =   Maximum training: Stallings's "Effective Use of Time" Workshops plus training in the comprehension strategy.

X_2 =   Minimum training: Stallings's "Effective Use of Time" Workshops

Sample

Thirty-four junior and senior high school teachers and their students from three suburban school districts in _____ will participate in the study. There will be three groups: a maximally trained group of 14 teachers, and an untrained group of 7 teachers. The three groups are further described in Table 3. All subjects will be volunteers and will vary in their prior training to teach reading.

Table 3. Subjects

Maximum-Training Subjects	Minimum-Training Subjects	Untrained Subjects
7 junior high teachers of Language Arts and English from District 1	7 junior high teachers of Language Art and English from District 2	7 junior high teachers of Language Arts and English from District 1
7 senior high from a variety of content areas from District 3	7 senior high from a variety of content areas from District 3	

Assignment to the three groups will vary for the senior and junior high teachers. Junior high teachers from one district will be assigned to the minimal-training condition and junior high teachers from another district will be assigned the maximal-training condition. Untrained teachers will be from one of these two districts. Assignment of senior high teachers will be determined by which night subjects sign up to take the workshops. Tuesday has been designated as the minimal-training condition; and Wednesday evening, the maximal-training condition.

When the study was first planned, senior high subjects were to be English teachers with some responsibility for teaching remedial reading. However, teachers who volunteered for the study come from a variety of content areas. For this reason, training for the senior high teachers will be modified to be applicable to reading expository text in content areas. Training for the subgroups of junior high teachers will focus on remedial readers' comprehension of expository text.

Treatments

The Strategy. The reading comprehension instruction strategy is a four-step strategy designed to improve secondary readers' comprehension of expository text by (a) activating and organizing the reader's prior knowledge, (b) structuring the material that the student is to read, and (c) providing an opportunity for the student to integrate the new information into his/her existing knowledge.

The strategy was developed as follows:

1. A review of the literature to determine the best methods for improving reading comprehension was conducted. The findings of the review were presented in Part II.

2. The strategy and accompanying teacher lesson plan were developed. The lesson plan is shown in Appendix A. (Appendix A is not included here. Interested readers can find material presented in it in the completed dissertation.) As a check on content validity, four experts in reading and former classroom teachers reviewed the strategy and lesson plan. All four express the opinion that the strategy should facilitate comprehension and that it should be possible for teachers to implement after training. As a result of the reviewers' comments, two modifications were made. One part of Step 1, categorizing information students had brainstormed, was dropped. Two experts felt it would be too difficult to implement and may not always be applicable. Another part of the Step 1, providing background information, was expanded on the lesson plan to enable the teacher to include plans for instruction. Minor changes in wording to clarify meaning were also made.

3. The strategy was field tested with students in _____ School District classroom. Students participated in each step of the strategy and easily filled in the overview. The field testing confirmed the decision to drop the categorizing activity. It took too much class time and was not necessary to ensure comprehension.

Training Teachers in the Strategy. Training teachers to use the comprehension instruction strategy will occur as part of Stallings's inservice program "Effective Use of Time Training." Both the minimum-treatment group and maximum-treatment group will participate in this program, which consists of five workshops that provide extensive training in instructional management. See Table 4 for a description of each workshop. The variation in training will occur during the fifth workshop and a sixth one added for the purpose of this study. The control group will receive no training.

Maximum-treatment group. The maximally trained teachers will participate in Stallings's program. They will receive training in one comprehension instruction strategy during the fifth workshop and a sixth one added for the purpose of this study. The following is the plan for the workshops:

Workshop 5

    1. Present the theoretical and research base for the strategy.

    2. Present an overview of the strategy by going over the summary.

    3. Model the strategy. The reading passage on which the modeling will be based will be determined after meeting the participants and identifying their specific needs. It may be different for the junior and senior high teachers.

    4. Discuss the reactions of the participants to the strategy.

              Ask: What do you like about the strategy?
                   Can you use the strategy? How?
                   What areas may be difficult to
                   implement?

    5. Go over illustrations of the strategy that are included in the homework packet. The packet is shown in Appendix B. (Appendix B is not included here. Interested readers can find material presented in it in the completed dissertation.)

    6. Have participants make a commitment to try the strategy with the lesson plan they prepared in class.

Table 4. Maximum and Minimum Training Treatments

Workshop Sequence	Minimal Training--Stallings's "Effective Use of Time" Workshops	Maximum Training--Stallings's "Effective Use of Time" Workshops + Training in the Comprehension Strategy.
Workshop 1	Research in Findings of Effective Use of Time -present research on effective use of time -analyze profiles -make commitment to try new ideas	Same
Workshop 2	Improving Classroom Organization -discuss what teachers tried in their classrooms -share good ideas on organizing -discuss grouping for instruction -arrange peer observations	Same
Workshop 3	Improving Interactions -discuss peer observation data discuss types of interactions teacher had i.e., levels of questions, feedback provided, checking for understanding	Same
Workshop 4	Improving Behavior Management -look at student off-task behavior from peer observation data -discuss control systems	Same
Workshop 5	Improving Instruction and Monitoring -discuss homework materials on instructing and monitoring: includes linking prior knowledge to new information, structured overviews, checks for understanding -present overview of diagnostic tests and reading in the content areas -discuss individual profiles and improvement -make commitments for continued change	Improving Instruction and Monitoring -present theoretical base for strategy -model strategy -discuss reactions to strategy -discuss examples -make commitment to try strategy
Workshop 6	None	Improving Instruction - continued -discuss implementation of strategy -discuss variations in implementation -prepare a lesson using the strategy -make commitment to try the strategy again -discuss individual profiles and improvement -make commitment for continued change

Participants will have a packet of information and
assignments to read before each session. Packet 1 will
contain the following information:

1. A brief discussion of the theoretical underpinnings
of the strategy

2. A strategy summary

3. Two blank lesson plans

4. Examples of the strategy applied to a variety of
reading selections.

Packet #2 will contain the following information:

1. Two short selections for completing a homework
assignment

2. Blank lesson plans

3. Variations of methods for assessing and activating
prior knowledge

Minimum-treatment group. The minimum-treatment group
also will participate in Stallings's program. The group
will participate in Workshop 5 of the regular program,
which includes the following activities:
1. Discuss homework readings and share ideas about
instructing and monitoring, graphic organizers, and
checking for understanding.
2. Present an overview of diagnostic reading tests and
content area reading.
3. Discuss individual profiles and personal
improvement.
4. Make a commitment for continued change.
The minimum-treatment group also will be introduced to
the theoretical underpinnings of the comprehension
instruction strategy. Participants will discuss articles
that present the concept of linking prior knowledge to new
information and that illustrate graphic organizers.
Teachers will share ideas on ways they may apply the ideas
in their classroom.
The maximum treatment differs from the minimum
treatment in that the concepts discussed in the minimum
treatment will be formally presented and then discussed in
the maximum treatment. The comprehension instruction
strategy, which is a classroom application of the concepts,
will be modeled only in the maximum treatment.
Furthermore, only teachers in the maximum treatment will
practice using the strategy in their classrooms and discuss
problems they may have implementing it.

<u>No-treatment group</u>. The no-treatment group will not participate in Stallings's program nor will they be introduced to the comprehension instruction strategy. This group was added to the study to provide baseline information on a student performance measure, namely: teachers will be asked to teach a designated reading lesson on which student comprehension will be measured. The measure will be administered posttreatment, but not pretreatment. The no-treatment group will constitute an improvised pretreatment condition because the measure will involve untrained teachers.

   <u>Pilot test</u>. A pilot of the maximum-treatment condition was conducted with participants in the fifth session of a recent inservice offering of Stallings's program. The training session included:

   1. Presentation of the theoretical and research basis of the strategy.

   2. An overview of the strategy.

   3. Modeling of the strategy with a reading selection (see appendix B).

   4. Discussion of illustrations of the strategy with other reading selections (see Appendix B).

   5. Discussion of participants' reactions.

   Teachers responded favorably to the strategy. They indicated that they felt it was practical, easy to incorporate into their existing teaching practices, and something they would implement. No modification has been made as a result of the pilot.

   <u>Trainers.</u> Jane Stallings will conduct training in all the "Effective Use of Time" workshops attended by the minimum-treatment group. I will not attend any of these sessions. Stallings will conduct the first four workshops of the "Effective Use of Time" program for the maximum-treatment group, and I will conduct the fifth and sixth workshops. I will be present during the first four workshops so that participants will know me and feel comfortable sharing ideas and problems.

<u>Measures</u>

   <u>The Strategy Observation Checklist</u>. Implementation of the strategy will be measured by observing each participant in the maximum- and minimum-training groups during three class periods before training and during three class periods after training. All six observations will occur

with one class selected by the teacher. To avoid observer bias, several different observers will conduct the six observations of each teacher. The untrained group will be observed once during the post-training observation week.

During each classroom observation of the maximum- and minimum-treatment teachers, observers will complete Stallings's Secondary Observations Instrument, which records classroom processes. One section of the instrument, the Classroom Snapshot, records how the teacher and aides spend their time and the activities in which students are engaged. The other section, the Five-Minute Interaction (FMI), records the teacher's verbal interactions and nonverbal behaviors for five five-minute time periods within a class period (Stallings and Mohlman, 1982). Immediately following the observation, observers complete a daily log in which they describe the day's lesson content and structure and provide explanations for unusual or noteworthy occurrences.

For the purposes of this study, a checklist has been added to Stallings' Secondary Observation Instrument. .This checklist is shown in Appendix C. (Appendix C is not included here. Interested readers can find material presented in it in the completed dissertation.) After each five-minute interaction (FMI), the observer will complete the strategy observation checklist to record the occurrence of any target instructional behaviors. In the daily log, observers will describe how the target behaviors were implemented.

During one post-observation, teachers will be given the same reading selection and asked to teach a reading lesson based on their recent training. Untrained teachers will be asked to teach it in their usual manner. In addition to completing the Secondary Observation Instrument and strategy checklist, the observers will tape the lesson.

Data from the pre- and post-training observations will be analyzed to determine the extent to which teachers implemented elements of the strategy. The Checklist will record the occurrence of seven variables: (1) brainstorming, (2) other checks for prior knowledge, (3) developing vocabulary, (4) providing background information, (5) use of a graphic organizer, (6) use of an outline, and (7) categorizing information.

Analysis of each five-minute interaction in which a target behavior occurred will supply information about the interactions that occurred during implementation and the duration of the instruction. For example: the FMI will show whether literal questions were asked when teachers used a graphic organizer or the amount of time that a teacher spent developing vocabulary. Additionally, the FMI will yield information about implementation that is not included on the checklist. For example, training in the strategy encourages teachers to ask higher cognitive questions. Frequency of higher cognitive questions is measured by the FMI. The tape recordings will provide an additional method for observing implementation. The recordings may provide information about implementation not shown on the checklist or the FMI.

Observers were trained in January in a six-day training session in _____. The seven observers are classroom teachers or supervisory personnel from two of the three participating school districts. Jane Stallings trained observers to use her Secondary Observation Instrument, and I trained them to use the Strategy Observation Checklist. Training included: definition of the target behaviors; presentation and discussion of examples and non-examples of the behaviors; and viewing a videotape of the strategy. (See Appendix C for training materials.)

Observers took a test at the end of the training to establish interrater reliability and accuracy of behavior identification. Observers watched two five-minute segments of a videotape of the strategy. For each segment they completed a five-minute interaction for the strategy checklist and the daily log. Observer reliability on the FMI was .90. The percentage of observer agreement on the checklist ranged from 70% to 100% with a mean of 80%. An analysis of discrepancies and a discussion with observers revealed that difficulty in identification of behaviors arose because the five-minute segments of the tape were out of the context of the entire lesson. For example, one segment showed the instructor helping students complete a graphic organizer. The observers did not see him discuss or pass out the organizer, but only asking questions and listing student responses under headings on the chalkboard. Some observers identified this behavior as an instance of categorizing, while others called it using a graphic organizer. Upon seeing a longer, more complete segment of the tape, all identified the use of the graphic organizer. Observers felt they could identify the behaviors more easily in the context of an entire class period of instruction.

Since post-training observations will not occur until May, a day-long review session with observers is planned in late April.

Student measures. To measure the effect of the instructional strategy on student comprehension, a domain-referenced test will be administered after students read a designated selection. The test will ask students to write down everything they can remember about the selection and to answer two questions that require more than recall of information. This type of test is similar to tests used by researchers in studies of schema theory.

The reading levels of students will be determined by

existing test scores or by a test administered at the
beginning of the second semester of school. The reading
level of the test selection will be determined from an
average of those scores. If the range of student reading
abilities varies greatly, tests at more than one reading
level will be developed.

On a designated observation day, teachers will be asked
to have students read the test selection, provide
instruction as usual, and then administer the
domain-referenced test. Data yielded by the tests will be
analyzed to determine whether students of teachers who
implemented the instructional strategy had higher
comprehension scores than students of untrained teachers.

Data Analysis

The Strategy Observation Checklist yields 7 scores.
The teachers' scores for the first three observations will
be averaged to a yield set of 7 mean pre-training scores.
The teachers' scores on the next three observations will be
similarly averaged to yield a set of 7 mean post-training
scores. Descriptive statistics for the scores of the
minimum-treatment and maximum-treatment teachers will be
computed. Analysis of covariance on each of the
post-training scores, using pre-training scores as the
covariate, will be done to determine whether the
maximum-treatment group implements each element of the
comprehension instruction strategy at a higher level than
the minimum-treatment group.

Student scores on each subtest (free recall and
short-answer) of the domain-referenced test will be
computed. Scorers will be trained to a criterion of .80
reliability. Descriptive statistics for the
maximum-treatment, minimum-treatment, and no-treatment
group of students will be computed. Analysis of covariance
of the subtest scores, using pre-training reading
achievement scores as the covariate, will be done to
determine whether maximum-treatment-group students perform
at a higher level than minimum-treatment-group students and
no-treatment-group students.

Time Line

November - December

1. Develop instructional strategy.
2. Develop observation instrument and observer training
   manual.
3. Establish validity of strategy.

January 3-7

1. Videotape implementation of the strategy in the
   classrooms.
2. Field test the strategy.

January 10-19

1. Train observers in _____.
2. Pilot test training.

January 19 - February 28

1. Observers make pre-intervention observations.
2. Develop teacher training workshops. Prepare
   presentations and materials to be given teachers.

March 1 - April 10

1. Stallings's Effective Use of Time" Workshops will
   occur. Each week for five weeks, teachers in the
   minimum- and maximum-treatment groups will attend a
   sixth workshop. The researcher will attend all
   workshops with the maximum-treatment group and conduct
   the last two workshops.

April

1. Review training session for observers.

May

1. Post-training observations.
2. Posttest administered to students.

May - June

1. Analyze data.

BIBLIOGRAPHY

Anderson, L. <u>Principles of small group instruction in elementary reading</u>. Paper presented at the International Reading Association Convention, Chicago, 1982.

Anderson, L., Evertson, C., & Brophy, J. An experimental study of effective teaching in first-grade reading groups. <u>Elementary School Journal</u>, 1979, <u>79</u>, 193-223.

Anderson, R.C., Pichert, J.W., & Shirey, L.L. <u>Effects of the reader's schema at different points in time</u>. (Technical Report No. 119) Urbana: University of Illinois, Center for the Study of Reading, April, 1979.

Anderson, R.C., Reynolds, R.E., Schallert, D.L., & Goetz, E.T. Frameworks for comprehending discourse. <u>American Educational Journal</u>, 1979, <u>14</u>, 367-381.

Anderson, R.C., Spiro, R.J. & Anderson, M.C. Schemata as scaffolding for the representation of information in connected discourse. <u>American Educational Research Journal</u>, 1978, <u>15</u>, 433-440.

Armbruster, B.B. & Anderson, T.H. <u>The effect of mapping on the free recall of expository text</u>. (Technical Report No. 160) Urbana: University of Illinois, Center for the Study of Reading, February, 1980.

Ausubel, D.P. In defense of advance organizers: A reply to the critics. <u>Review of Educational Research</u>, 1978, <u>48</u>, 251-257.

Baker, L., & Anderson, R.I. Effects of inconsistent information on text processing: Evidence for comprehension monitoring. <u>Reading Research Quarterly</u>, 1982, <u>17</u>, 281-293.

Baker, L. & Brown, A.L. <u>Metacognitive skills and reading</u>. (Technical Report No. 188) Urbana: University of Illinois, Center for the Study of Reading, November, 1980. (ERIC Document Service No. ED 195 932).

Bransford, J.D., & McCarrell, N. A sketch of cognitive
    approach to comprehension: Some thoughts about
    understanding what it means to comprehend. In W.B.
    Weemer and D.S. Palermo (Eds.). <u>Cognition and the
    symbolic process</u>. Hillsdale, N.J.: Erlbaum, 1975.

Bransford, J.D., Stein, B.S., Shelton, T.S., & Owings,
    R.A. Cognition and adaptation: The importance of
    learning to learn. In J. Harvey, (Ed.), <u>Cognition,
    Social Behavior and the Environment</u>. Hillsdale, N.J.:
    Erlbaum, 1980.

Cramer, Eugene. One more time: Every teacher a teacher of
    reading. <u>Curriculum Review,</u> 1978, <u>17</u>, 391-383

Crawford, J., Gage, N., Corno, L., Stayrook, N., Mitman,
    A., Schunk, D., Stallings, J., Baskin, E., Harvey, P.,
    Austin, D., Cronin, D., & Newman, R. <u>An experiment on
    teacher effectiveness and parent-assisted instruction
    in the third grade</u>. (3 Vols.). Stanford, Calif.:
    Center for Educational Research at Stanford, 1978.

Dansereu, D.F. Development and evaluation of a learning
    strategy training program. <u>Journal of Educational
    Psychology</u>, 1979, <u>71</u>, 64-73.

Duffy, G., & McIntyre, L. <u>A qualitative analysis of how
    various primary grade teachers employ the structured
    learning component of the direct instruction model when
    teaching reading.</u> (Research Series No. 80) East
    Lansing: Institute for Research on Teaching, Michigan
    State University, June, 1980.

Dunkin M., & Biddle, B. <u>The study of teaching</u>. New York:
    Holt, Rinehard and Winston, 1974.

Durkin, D. Reading comprehension instruction in five basal
    reading series. <u>Reading Research Quarterly</u>, 1981, <u>16</u>,
    515-544.

Good, T. & Grouws, D. The Missouri mathematics
    effectiveness project: An experimental study in
    fourth-grade classrooms. <u>Journal of Educational
    Psychology</u>, 1979, <u>71</u>, 335-362.

Graves, M.F. & Clark, D.L. The effect of adjunct
    questions on high school low achievers' reading
    comprehension. <u>Reading Improvement</u>, 1981, <u>18</u>, 8-13.

Holliday, W.G. & Harvey, D.A. Adjunct labeled drawings in teaching physics to junior high school students. Journal of Research in Science Teaching, 1976, 13, 37-43.

Langer, J.A. Facilitating text processing: The elaboration of prior knowledge. In J.A. Langer and M.T. Burke (Eds.), Reader meets author/Bridging the gap. Newark: International Reading Association, 1982, 149-162.

Langer, J.A. From theory to practice: A Prereading plan. Journal of Reading, 1981, 25, 152-156.

Meyer, B.J.F. The organization of prose and its effects on memory. Amsterdam: North Holland, 1975. Meyer, B.J.F., Brandt, D.H., & Bluth, G.F. Use of top-level structure in text: Key for reading comprehension of ninth grade students. Reading Research Quarterly, 1980, 16, 72-103.

Mohlman, G.G. Assessing the impact of three inservice training models. Paper presented at the annual meeting of the American Educational Research Association. New York, 1982.

Mohlman, G.G., Coladarci, T., & Gage, N.L. Comprehension and attitude as predictors of implementation of teacher training. Journal of Teacher Education, 1982, 33, 31-36.

Pearson, P.D., Hansen, J., & Gordon, C. The effect of background knowledge on young children's comprehension of explicit and implicit information. (Technical Report No. 116). Urbana: University of Illinois, Center for the Study of Reading, March, 1979.

Pearson, P.D. & Kamil, M.L. Basic processes and instructional practices in teaching reading. (Reading Education Report No. 7). Urbana: University of Illinois, Center for the Study of Reading, December, 1978.

Rumelhart, D. & Ortony, A. The representation of knowledge in memory. In R.C. Anderson, R.J. Spiro, & W.E. Montague (Eds.). Schooling and the acquisition of knowledge. Hillsdale, N.J.: Erlbaum Associates, 1977, 90-135.

Singer, H., & Ruddell, R. (Eds.), Theoretical models and processes of reading. Newark, Del.: International Reading Association, 1976.

Slinger, E. A systematic observation of the extent to which students in secondary content area classrooms are given instruction in reading assigned material. Unpublished dissertation, University of Oregon, 1981.

Stallings, J.A. Effective use of time program, Unpublished training manual, 1982.

Stallings, J.A. Changing teacher behavior: A challenge for the 1980's. Paper presented to the American Education Research Association, Los Angeles, California, April, 1981.

Stallings, J.A. How to change the process of teaching reading in secondary schools. Educational Horizons, 1979, 57, 196-201.

Stallings, J.A. The process of teaching basic reading skills in secondary schools. Report submitted to the National Institute of Education, December, 1980.

Stallings, J.A. & Kaskowitz, D.H. Follow through classroom observation evaluation, 1972-1973. Menlo Park, Calif.: Stanford Research Institute, 1974.

Stallings, J.A., & Mohlman, G.G. Effective use of time in secondary reading classrooms. Paper presented to the International REading Association, Chicago, Ill., April, 1982.

Stallings, J.A., Needels, M., & Stayrook, N. The teaching of basic reading skills in secondary schools, phase II and phase III. SRI Interntaional, Menlo Park, California, 1979.

Thelen, J. Improving reading in science. Newark: International Reading Association, 1976.

Vacca, R.T. Development of a functional reading strategy: Implications for content area instruction. Journal of Educational Research, 1975, 69.

Vaughan, J.L. Instructional strategies and adolescent readers: Research Revelations. Unpublished paper, September 1981. To be included in A. Burger & H.A. Robinson (Eds.). Secondary school reading: What research reveals for classroom practices. Urbana: National Council of Teachers of English, in press.

Vaughan, J.L. Use construct to improve active reading and learning. Journal of Reading, 1982, 25, 412-422.

Willmore, D.J. A comparison of four methods of studying, A college textbook. Unpublished doctoral dissertation, University of Minnesota, 1967.

Wooster, G.F. Teaching the SQ3R method of study: An investigation of the instructional approach. Unpublished doctoral dissertation, Ohio State University, 1958.

Wyne, M.D., & Stuck, G.G. Time on-task and reading performance in underachieving children. Journal of Reading Behavior, 1979, 11, 119-128.

Neal B. Strudler

<u>Dissertation Proposal</u>

The Role of School-based Computer Coordinators as
Change Agents in Elementary School Programs

Information about the completed dissertation is in
<u>Dissertation Abstracts International</u>, vol. 48, no. 11,
section A, Page 2853.
The DAI order number is DA 8800554.

INTRODUCTION

Purpose of the Study

The purpose of this study is to examine the role of school-based computer specialists as change agents in elementary school programs. The study replicates aspects of the research project <u>Patterns of Successful Assistance in Urban School Improvement Programs</u> (Miles, Saxl, and Lieberman 1985) conducted at the Center for Policy Research and Teachers College, Columbia University.

Background

<u>The Need for Teacher Training</u>. The Rand Change Agent Study (Berman and McLaughlin, 1977) found that even the best innovation could not succeed with inadequately trained or uncommitted teachers. Staff development, therefore, is critical for the implementation of new programs and teaching methods. One element of effective staff development is support following initial training (Gall and Renchler, 1985). Follow-up support helps teachers to transfer newly learned teaching skills and practices into their active teaching repertoire (Joyce and Showers, 1983). The present study will examine the computer specialist's role in facilitating the transfer of teacher training with regard to instructional computing.

Arthur Luehrmann (1984) and other proponents of computer programming instruction have argued that computers can be most efficiently implemented through specialized classes with a limited number of specially trained teachers. Where the goal is implementation of computers throughout the curriculum, however, training demands are greatly increased (Mounsund, 1985). The present study focuses on the training demands that are involved when the goal is integration of computers throughout the curriculum.

<u>The Role of Instructional Computer Coordinator</u>. A growing number of people hold the position of instructional computer coordinator at the school level (Barbour, 1985; Moursund, 1985). A recent survey in <u>Electronic Learning</u> found the following regarding school-based computer coordinators:

1. Job descriptions vary greatly.

2. Only 21 percent of the respondents actually hold the title "computer coordinator"; many others function in that role on a de facto basis.

3. 80 percent of school computer specialists fulfill their role as an additional responsibility; only 4 percent function on a part-time or "released" basis.

The present study will attempt a detailed description of the computer specialist's role. It will focus on the emerging group of specialists who have been provided released time to facilitate computer implementation in the schools.

The Change Agent Role. A recent study of school improvement found that the successful implementation of innovative programs is dependent upon the intervention of key personnel involved in various change agent roles (Huberman and Crandall, 1982). A change agent is defined as an assistance person whose role includes responsibility for facilitating change. In the present study, the change agents are local consultants or trainers who are released from full-time teaching loads to provide a variety of services on a school level.

This emerging role is being given increased attention because of a shift in the approach to school improvement. Whereas the post-Sputnik school reform campaign tended to rely on centralized curriculum changes, current efforts focus on school-based change. With this change there has been a corresponding shift in change agent roles from a disseminator of ideas and materials to a process consultant (Beaton, 1985).

While change agents are widely used as "special assisters" in current school improvement programs, little is known about their functions, the strategies they employ, the specific skills most crucial for success, or how to train for such skills (Fullan, 1981; Miles et al., 1985). The Patterns of Successful Assistance study (Miles et al., 1985) focused on these concerns in its two-year investigation of 17 change agents working in three urban school improvement programs. Miles and his colleagues developed a list of strategies that change agents use (Appendix A, Part 1), skills that they need (Appendix A, Part 2), and outcomes that they intend to effect (Appendix A, Part 3). This list of strategies, skills, and outcomes will be used in the present study to investigate the role of computer specialists.

Beaton (1985) replicated aspects of the Patterns of Successful Assistance study in focusing on the role staff

development specialists in three school improvement
programs in the Northwest and the outcomes they achieve.
We found that these specialists use a combination of
product- and client-centered strategies that require
sophisticated interpersonal skills. The main teacher
outcomes he reported were motivation, positive attitudes,
and enhanced communication and cooperation between
teachers.

The present study seeks to extend the findings of Miles
and his colleagues and Beaton. It is my intent to
replicate aspects of their studies to investigate a new
change agent role: the school-based computer specialist.

The Setting: Eugene District 4J

In 1984, the District 4J Computer Council recognized
the need for a uniform approach to computer education at
the elementary level. In June of that year, a group of
teachers, under the direction of the District Computer
Coordinator, began developing a program that would focus on
integrating the computer into the established curriculum
and on providing articulation between grade levels. The
program was piloted during the 1984-85 school year. The
pilot study was evaluated (Ames, Gilberstad, Sky, and
Strudler, 1985) and deemed feasible contingent upon
continued district support with regard to computer
resources and staff development. The evaluators
recommended that part-time "computer persons" be designated
to coordinate training, maintenance, and scheduling at the
school level.

During the 1984-85 school year, only one of Eugene's 24
elementary school employed a released-time computer
specialist (defined as any specialist who is assigned .1FTE
or greater for computer-related responsibilities). By the
following school year, nine elementary schools had opted
for released specialists. The present study will examine
the situational and historical context of this trend.

Significance of Study

This study has the promise of contributing to the
effectiveness of implementation of computers in education.
Knowledge of the computer specialist's role may help school
districts and other planners to formulate policies and
procedures that guide allocation of these personnel.
Information on successful strategies used by computer
specialists might increase their effectiveness as change
agents and enable their supervisors to provide better
guidance and support. Furthermore, identification of the

skills required in that role could aid in the selection and training of prospective specialists. Ultimately, knowledge of the role of school-based computer specialists would increase the likelihood that resources committed to instructional computing would lead to successful implementation.

Research Questions

This study will investigate the activities of school-based computer specialists with regard to their effort to facilitate change in their schools. In particular, it sets out to answer the following five questions:

1. What is the situational and historical context in which computer specialists do their work?

2. What is the range of strategies used by computer specialists?

3. What skills do they need in that role?

4. What are the intended and actual accomplishments resulting from the computer specialist's work?

5. What frustrations and rewards do computer specialists experience?

METHOD

Research Design

This is an exploratory case study that will use
questionnaire, interview, and observation procedures to
survey two or three change agents carrying out a
school-level computer specialist role. The study
represents the first stage of the
descriptive-correlational-experimental loop that has been
used to guide research on teaching (Rosenshine & Furst,
1973). In this first stage, the purpose is to identify
potentially effective strategies and skills used by
computer specialists. In subsequent studies, variations in
use of these strategies and skills can be correlated with
effectiveness criteria such as the degree of teachers' use
of computers. Finally, effective strategies and skills
identified in the second phase can be incorporated into a
training program. Then, experimental research can be
conducted to test the training program and determine the
causal connections between strategies and skills used and
actual outcomes.
In this study, descriptive data will be gathered from
multiple sources using multiple measures. Responses of the
specialists will be checked against those of other
informants, namely, their supervisors (principals and the
District Computer Coordinator) and clients (the teachers in
their school). Observation of representative activities
and examination of relevant documents will provide an
additional validity check.

Sample

Eugene District 4J currently has nine elementary
schools with released-time computer specialists. A sample
of two or three of these schools will be selected for this
study. The sample will be obtained by consulting with the
District Computer Coordinator, the District Evaluation
Specialist, the Lane Educational Service District
Curriculum/Staff Development Specialist, and university
professors in educational computing and research methods.
Specialists will be chosen from schools that have been
identified as having a high degree of implementation of
instructional computing. Additionally, consideration will
be given to choosing specialists who vary with regard to
critical variables, namely: (1) technical expertise in

computing, (2) role expectations of computer specialists by
supervisors, teachers, and themselves, (3) previous
teaching experience in the particular school, and (4)
available resources. A brief description of prospective
members of the sample follows:

School A participated in the 4J elementary pilot study
last year. Mary G., the computer specialist, is currently
.5 computer-related and .5 Physical Education instructor.
Mary is in her first year as released-time specialist,
though she has served similar roles in past years while not
released from classroom responsibilities. Mary was release
part-time last year to serve as a curriculum writer for the
pilot elementary computer curriculum.

School A has the distinction of being chosen as a test
site for using and evaluating Sunburst problem-solving
software; this arrangement will continue for at least two
years. Mary was clearly instrumental in "leading the way"
at School A, while also managing to create a great deal of
teacher involvement and support. Mary clearly sees herself
as a staff developer and not a "computer teacher."

School B participated in the 4J elementary pilot study
last year. Tom K., the computer specialist, is currently
in his second year (.5 FTE) at this school. Tom was hired
from "out of staff" after the School B faculty and
principal supported the need for the position. Last spring
I observed at School B and found that Tom was serving to a
large degree as the "computer teacher," a role that he
served well. This year Tom's goal has been to wean School
B of his services. In addition to his responsibilities at
School B, Tom has been hired by the District Office to work
on formulating the district's problem-solving curriculum
guide.

School C participated in the 4J elementary pilot study
last year. Annie K. is currently in her first year as a
released computer specialist. Annie is a kindergarten
teacher (.5 FTE) and was released as computer specialist
for an additional .2 FTE. School C's faculty and principal
decided to take the .2 allotted and create a .4 position
for half a year. Annie's tenure as specialist ends by
spring break. While this situation might make it difficult
to include this case, Annie's inclusion would contrast one
critical variable: the importance of technical expertise.
While Annie is more advanced than a "computer novice," she
is clearly not at the technical level of what I would
categorize a "specialist." I would imagine that her
"people skills" and established relationships with faculty
members compensate a good deal for her lack of computer
experience. Annie's lack of technical expertise would be
interesting to contrast with the other cases. Also, it
would be interesting to view Annie's role after her tenure
as specialist expires.

I also will survey the remaining six schools in order

to determine the situational context of their computer specialist role. this procedure will be useful for determining the representativeness of the sample.

Data Collection Instruments

Semi-structured interviews and a questionnaire will be adapted from those used in the studies of Miles, (1985) and Beaton (1985). Informants will include the computer specialists, their supervisors (principals, district administrators), and their clients (teachers). Further data will be gathered by observation and document analysis.

Two forms of the questionnaire will be used to determine whether each computer specialist used particular strategies and skills, and effected particular outcomes. One (see appendix B) will serve as a checklist to create a profile of typical strategies, skills, and outcomes for each specialist; the other, almost identical, asks each supervisor to prepare a similar profile of each specialist.

Four interview schedules will be used. The interview with supervisors (see Appendix C) will seek the computer program's history and policy, and then will ask about how each trainer developed and used his/her specialist skills.
Specialists will be interviewed twice. The first interview (see Appendix D) will ask about a typical day of a computer specialist and probe into the outcomes and future directions associated with that role. The second interview (see Appendix E) with specialists asks about strategies and skills typically used in their work. It also seeks to identify what skills they bring into the job, what development of skills has occurred since that time, and how the learning process occurred.
Teachers will be interviewed (see Appendix F) concerning their involvement with computers in their school. They will be asked about the strategies and skills of the specialists and encouraged to describe specific incidents in which the specialist was especially helpful to them. They also will talk about the outcomes of the computer specialist's work and their opinions of the skills needed for that role.
In addition, relevant documents will be examined, and observations will be conducted of workshops, conferences, and planning activities.

Data Analysis

Interviews will be tape-recorded and selected segments will be transcribed. Field notes and interview data will

be coded for analysis according to the list of variables
(see Appendix A) developed by Matthew Miles. Some codes
will be added and others dropped in the light of the data
gathered. Coding will be tested for inter-rater
reliability.

All data handling will be done using AppleWorks
integrated software and an Apple IIc microcomputer with
512k extended memory. The extended memory will enable
large files of data to be searched for codes or key words.
The ability to have several files on the AppleWorks
"desktop" at one time will enable vignettes from interviews
to be transferred into the text of the report without the
risk of error involved in retyping.

Analysis will commence with grouping of similarly coded
items, allowing for testing and elimination of doubtful
coding. Data then will be analyzed case by case using
Miles' constructs as a structure for the reporting. In
addition, data will be compared across cases. Finally, the
results will be compared with those of Miles and his
colleagues (1985) and Beaton (1985).

Time Line

March: -- Get proposal approval from university and
               District 4J.
            -- Adjust Miles' instrumentation for present
               study.

April-   -- Gather historical data from district.
June: -- Gather data at chosen sites.

June-
August: -- Analyze data, begin writing.

Fall
Quarter: -- Finish writing in Fall '86.

APPENDIX A

VARIABLES USE IN THE STUDY

1. Strategies Used by Change Agents

A strategy is defined as a carefully planned method of translating theory and assumptions into action in order to achieve a goal. The classification of strategies is based on the system developed by Matthew Miles (1984). The fifteen strategies are defined as follows:

Providing technical mastery: helping individuals develop competence in specific techniques.

Resource linking: a dissemination process that involves transmitting ideas from outside researchers and trainers and building them into a teacher's repertoire of skills through on-going training; or introducing clients with needs to resource people.

Solution giving: providing innovation or other products of research as solutions to the perceived needs of others, often initiated without negotiation.

Training of groups: running workshops and courses to teach understandings and skills.

Coaching of individuals: training and teaching 1-1 using clinical observation and conferences in the teacher's classroom.

Demonstrating, modeling: demonstrating skills or techniques to assist understanding and to serve as a model for the learners to copy.

Energizing, motivating: initiating awareness and involvement; building confidence and a willingness to improve; establishing a rationale for the techniques being taught.

Supporting the client emotionally: relaxing tension and dispelling fear; reassuring and stressing positives with sensitivity and empathy.

Developing a support structure: creating a network or procedure for the support of clients, involving their teaching peers, their supervisors, or both.

Monitoring, evaluating: judging the effectiveness of a teacher's performance in order to stimulate change.

Networking among clients: building relationships between clients, helping them help each other, especially through peer coaching in this case.

Collaborative problem solving: shared involvement with clients in the problem-solving process.
Supported planning: assisting clients through the planning process.

Resource adding: supplying materials and ideas to clients.

Controlling client action: exercise of power, albeit expert power used with client consent, to direct the actions of clients.

2. Skills Use by Change Agents

Skills are defined as requisite knowledge or ability, or special qualifications to perform the tasks involved in the role. The focus in analyzing the data will be on attributes and capabilities of the change agent expressed with a qualitative description by informants; e. g. , the trainer does this well (or poorly). The classification of skills is based on the revised system developed by Miles and colleagues (1985). The eighteen skills are defined and illustrated as follows:

Interpersonal ease: relating simply and directly to others. Examples: Very open person... Can deal with people... Nice manner... Has always been able to deal with staff... You have to be able to work with people, know when to stroke, when to hold back, when to assent, know "which buttons to push,"... Gives individuals time to vent feelings, lets them know her interest in them... She can talk to anyone...

Group functioning: understanding group dynamics, able to facilitate teamwork. Examples: Has ability to get a group moving... He started with nothing and then made us come together as a united body... Good group facilitator... Lets the discussion flow.

Training/doing workshops: direct instruction, teaching adults in a systematic way. Examples: Gave workshops on how to develop plans... Taught us consensus method with five finger game... He prepares a great deal and enjoys it... He has the right chemistry and can impart knowledge at the peer level.

<u>Educational general (master teacher)</u>: wide educational
experience, able to impart skills to others. Examples:
Excellent teaching skills, taught all the grades, grade
leader work, resource teacher, has done staff development
with teachers... Title I programs where I was always
assisting, supporting, being resource person to teachers...
A real master teacher, much teacher training work.

<u>Educational content</u>: knowledge of school subject matter.
Examples: Demonstrating expertise in a subject area...
Parents thought kindergarten would be all academic. She
showed them the value of play, of trips... Knows a great
deal about teaching, especially reading. What she doesn't
know, she finds out.

<u>Technical expertise in computing</u>: (should I add this or
does it fit into the above? Should the above be modified?)

<u>Administrative/organizational</u>: defining and structuring
work, activities, time. Examples: Highly organized, has
everything prepared in advance... I could take an idea and
turn it into a program... Well organized, good at
prioritizing, scheduling, knows how to set things up.

<u>Initiative taking</u>: starting or pushing activities, moving
directly toward action. Examples: Assertive, clear sense
of what he wanted to do... Ability to poke and prod where
needed to get things done... I had to assert myself so he
didn't step on me.

<u>Trust/rapport-building</u>: developing a sense of safety,
openness, reduced threat on part of clients; good
relationship-building. Examples: A breath of fresh air.
In two weeks he had gained confidence of staff... She had
become one of the gang, eats lunch with them. A skilled
seducer (knows how to get people to ask for help)... I have
not repeated what they said, so trust was built... Even
those who knew everything before now let her help because
they aren't threatened... She was so open and understanding
that I stopped feeling funny.

<u>Support</u>: providing nurturant relationship, positive
affective relationship. Examples: Able to accept harsh
things teachers say. "It's OK, everyone has these
feelings"... A certain compassion for others. Always
patient, never critical, very enthusiastic.

<u>Confrontation</u>: direct expression of negative information
without generating negative affect. Examples: Can
challenge in a positive way... She will lay it on the line
about what works and what won't... He is talkative and

factual. His strength is being outspoken... He can point out things and get away with being blunt... Able to tell people they were wrong and they accept it.

Conflict mediation: resolving or improving situations where multiple incompatible interests are in play. Examples: Effected a compromise between upper- and lower-grade teachers on use of a checklist. Teachers resented the chair's autocratic behavior. So she spoke openly to him about it. Things have been considerably better... The principal is very vindictive. He was constantly mediating, getting her to soften her attitude... Can handle people who are terribly angry, unreasonable, keeps cool.

Collaboration: creating relationships where influence is mutually shared. Examples: Deals on the same level we do, puts in his ideas... I've never seen a time that teachers felt they were told to do something... Leads and directs us but not in a way like professors and students, but as peers. Doesn't judge us or put us down... Has ideas of her own, like in math, but flexible enough to maintain the teachers' way of doing things, too.

Confidence-building: strengthening client's sense of efficacy, belief in self. Examples: She makes all feel confident and competent. Doesn't patronize... "You can do it. " She'll help... He has a way of drawing out teachers' ideas. He injects a great deal but you feel powerful... She makes people feel like a million in themselves. Like a shot of adrenalin boosting your mind, ego, talents, and professional expertise... Her attitude: "try it, you'll like it. "

Diagnosing individuals: forming a valid picture of the needs/problems of an individual teacher or administrator as a basis for action. Examples: You need to realize that when a teacher says she has the worst class, that means "I need help. "... He has an ability to focus in on problems and get rid of the verbiage... picking up the real message... sensitive, looks at teacher priorities first... knows when an off-hand joke is a signal for help.

Diagnosing organizations: forming a valid picture of the needs/problems of a school as an organization (including its culture) as a basis for action. Examples: Analyzing a situation, recognizing problems, jumping ahead of where you are to where you want to go... When I analyzed beyond the surface, The way the principal was using meetings for administrative purposes... Anticipates problems schools face... Brought in report on reading/math and attendance, helped us know where we should be going... Helped team look at the data in the assessment package.

Managing/controlling: orchestrating the improvement process; coordinating activities, time and people; direct influence on others. Examples: She filled all the gaps in terms of legwork, preparing materials and coordinating our contact with school and district administrators... A task master and keeps the process going... Makes people do things rather than doing the process himself... He sets a pace, like the bouncing ball on songs.

Resource bringing: locating and providing information, materials, practices, equipment useful to clients. Examples; if it's broken, he fixes it. He uses his network to get us supplies... Brings ideas that she has seen work elsewhere... Had the newest research methods, articles ideas, waters it down for our needs... Brought manipulative materials for help with multiplication.

Demonstration: modeling new behavior in classrooms or meetings. Examples: He's a great story teller--gets the kids very interested... Willing to go into classrooms and take risks... Modelling... Was real, did demos with their classes... Watching someone else teach my class makes me reflect on what I'm doing... Showed the chair by his own behavior how to be more open.

3. Outcomes of the Change Agent Activities

Outcomes are considered to be anything in regard to teachers, students, administrators, or schools as a unit that result from the interventions of the change agents. The 10 outcomes, based on the classification of Miles (1984), are defined as follows:

Short-run success: small achievements made that enable other achievements; for example, the change agent provided resources in order to gain legitimacy.

Use of specific products: teachers use products or materials that they hadn't previously used.

Positive relationships: client satisfaction with positive relationship with the change agent.

Satisfaction with the program: positive attitudes of teachers and administrators toward the program.

Implementation of program: the extent to which the formal program is being carried out, usually by teachers being able to perform the new skills or techniques in their classroom.

<u>School climate change</u>: feelings, norms, sentiments have changed; e.g., there has been a change in the content of lunch table conversations.

<u>Organizational change</u>: changes in the structure or procedures of the school.

<u>Student impact</u>: students have a favorable attitude to the new teaching method, or have changed behavior in some way, or have changed in achievement.

<u>Capacity building</u>: improved capability or skills of teachers or school staff; staff are better at doing things.

<u>Institutionalization</u>: program features, structures, and procedures are built into the school.

<u>Energized, motivated clients</u>: (Retained by Beaton, dropped by Miles; I think this probably should be included): the clients have a desire for improving, and/or are enthused about the program.

APPENDIX B

PROFILE OF COMPUTER SPECIALISTS[1]

Please answer the following profile questions to give us a
picture (snapshot) of the way you work in your program. Try
to indicate which behaviors are most typical of you.

1.   Rank the following items on a scale of 1-5 and rank from
most typical (1) to least typical (5). Rank only those
descriptors that apply to you.

In general, your <u>main priorities</u> as an assistance person are
to:

_____ aid the improvement <u>process</u> in schools
        and/or individuals
_____ expand the <u>Knowledge</u> of clients
_____ bring <u>resources</u> to the client
_____ aid the change with the development of <u>products</u>
_____ other - please explain: _____

2. Select up to a total of 6 items that apply to you as an
assistance person and rank from <u>1</u> (most typical) to 6.

Your style is:

_____ manipulative   _____ situation-specific
_____ intuitive   _____ supportive
_____ active   _____ collaborative
_____ low key   _____ business-like
_____ facilitative   _____ expert as opposed
                                    to collegial
_____ reflective   _____ high key
_____ passive   _____ outgoing
_____ directive   _____ collegial as exposed to
                                    expert
_____ working alone   _____ systematic
_____ characterized by a   _____ characterized by a positive
        sense of humor   sense of self
_____ other: _____

_____

[1]Developed for the <u>Patterns of Successful Assistance</u> study
 and modified with permission.

3. Select up to a total of 6 items that apply to you as an assistance person and rank from 1 (most typical) to 6.

The following general skills are essential to the way you do your work:

_____ talking   _____ training, doing workshops
_____ listening   _____ master teacher
_____ interpersonal ease   _____ knowledge of educational
                                    content
_____ group functioning   _____ administrative/organization
_____ reading   _____ ability to take things
                                    with a "grain of salt"
_____ other:_____

4. Select up to a total of 6 items that apply to you as an assistance person and rank from 1 (most typical) to 6.

_____ initiative taking   _____ trust/rapport-building
_____ support   _____ confrontation
_____ conflict mediation   _____ collaboration
_____ confidence   _____ diagnosing individual
      building   needs
_____ managing/   _____ diagnosing school's needs
      controlling
_____ resource-bringing   _____ demonstration/modeling
_____ other: _____

5. Select up to a total of 6 items that apply to you as an assistance person and rank from 1 (most typical) to 6.

The following strategies are most often used by you:

_____ solution-giving   _____ providing technical
                                    assistance
_____ resource-adding   _____ energizing/motivating client
_____ resource-linking   _____ controlling client action
_____ re-educating client   _____ collaborative problem-
                                    solving
_____ supported planning   _____ developing support structure
_____ monitoring/   _____ supporting client
      evaluating   emotionally
_____ clinical 1-1   _____ other:_____
      conferencing

6. Select up to a total of 6 items that apply to you as an assistance person and rank from 1 (most typical) to 6.

The following outcomes have been realized due to your work:

_____ use of new products _____ short run successes/decisions

_____ program model implemented _____ satisfaction in relationship with clients

_____ school climate change _____ organizational change
_____ student impact _____ capacity building
_____ institutionalization of _____ too early to identify outcomes
  model
_____ energized/motivated other: _____
  clients vs. burnout

Your name _____ Date _____

Any comments you have about this profile:

APPENDIX C

OUTLINE OF INTERVIEW WITH SUPERVISOR

1. Background
   a. Name
   b. Job title (or role)
   c. How long have you been in this job?

2. First I'd like to recheck my understanding of where things stand with the program at the moment.
   a. Overview of project history
   b. Operating methods
   c. Role of computer specialist
   d. Ways in which teachers become involved
   e. Support for the program within the district
   f. Anything else I should know about the program at the moment?

3. Now for the rest of the time I'd like to take a careful look at the role of the computer specialist in your school.

   a. Can you give me a sketch of how _____ was functioning, what she was like at the point that you hired her? What were the strengths, the knowledge, the attitudes, and skills that you saw? (ASK FOR EXAMPLES, ILLUSTRATIONS)

   b. The next question is, what do you think _____ has learned during her time since assuming the computer specialist role? In what ways has she grown and developed, become more effective?

   c. Just how did this learning take place--what sources or mechanisms were involved? (Check for training, supervision, learning from experience, reading, partnerships, meetings, etc.). Maybe you can give me some specific examples or incidents to make it concrete.

   d. People vary a lot in the ways that they work in schools. Thinking of _____, what strategies or approaches would you say she's especially good at? Let's take a look at the profile you filled out for her (QUESTION 5). Could you give some examples or incidents that would illustrate the strategies that you ranked high (1,2, or 3) (GET AT LEAST 2 INCIDENTS.)

e.   And what would say are the strongest skills
     that _____ has? Here again, let's look at the
     profile (QUESTIONS 3 & 4). Can you give me some
     examples that would illustrate these skills,
     especially high ranking ones?

f.   Do you have any comments about the style
     of _____, especially the items you ranked
     highly on the profile (QUESTION 2).

g.   Anything else you'd like to tell me about _____

     that would give me a flavor of what is special or
     unique about <u>her</u> way of working?

4.   a.   Do you have any general comments or thoughts about
          what if takes to be an effective computer
          specialist in your school?

     b.   Which of these skills do you think are teachable
          and learnable, and which probably not--you just
          have to pick the right people in the first place?

     c.   If you were designing a training or learning
          program for computer specialists, what would the
          key ingredient be as far as you're concerned?

5.   Is there anything else you would like to add?

APPENDIX D

FIRST INTERVIEW WITH COMPUTER SPECIALIST

This interview is aimed at getting acquainted with your
activities. It is not an evaluation. It is a study of those
who have succeeded in implementing computers in schools.
The general idea is to get a realistic, concrete picture of
what you do and how you feel about it. This will help to
make clear what it takes to assist teachers with
instructional computer use.

1. Background
    a. Name
    b. Job title (or role)
    c. Thumbnail sketch of your job: what you do, who you
        work with
    d. How long have you been in this job?
        -- ask for educational and non-educational jobs
        preceding this one
        -- check for prior work with teaching adults,
        helping with change, etc.
    e. What's your educational background?
        -- where attended, level (formal ed.)
        -- non-degree training (workshops, courses, etc.)

2. Could you pick a day sometime this or last week that
    was reasonably typical, and tell me what you did that
    day?
    a. What happened first thing?
    b. And then? (Encourage movement through day; ask when
        things not clear)
    c. Are there any other types of activities in your job
        that didn't happen during this day?
        -- get brief description

3. a. Can you suggest some teachers at your school who
        might be good to speak with?
    b. Can you give me a brief history of your school's
        involvement with using computers?
    c. What was the status of computer use before you
        assumed your role?
    d. What caused your school to create the role of
        released computer specialist?
    e. Who assisted with computer-related duties before
        you assumed that role?

f. I'd like to know all about the various phases of
    implementation of computers in your school. (Make
    sure all these specific items are covered for each
    phase: time goals, priorities, what actually
    happened, approaches or strategies, problems and
    dilemmas (with specific examples), other people
    involved and what they did, key skills used by the
    computer specialist, and others.)

g. Now we're up to the present in the story of this
    school, could I ask you about what you think have
    been the results so far?
    -- get a list
    -- probe for how person knows this, what based on
    (if not clear)

h. Looking at these results, I'm wondering if you can
    say whether your work impacted on them directly--
    results where you can see that your work
    specifically made a difference. Any of them like
    that?
    -- note degree of certainty about impact of own
    work

f. What's your guess about what will happen next with
    the school in its work with computers (in the next
    few months)?

4. a. Could you describe what you think are the results
        so far regarding having relseased computer
        specialists in nine schools in the district?

   b. What do you anticipate will happen in the near
        future?

5. a. Anything else you think I should know at this time?

IALIST

ealistic a picture as

le you filled out about
ist.
escriptors of your
 example or an incident
llustrate those you

al skills.
fic skills.
egies.

ttle. For the rest of
u and your skills and
and people that you've
look at you and how
a computer specialist.
d like to get a good
has gone during your

ds: before you assumed
ur work in that role,
and later on.

2. As I recall it, you formally became your school's
   computer specialist _____ (date). Tell me about
   your involvement with instructional computing before
   you became a computer specialist.

   a. Can you think back to that point -- just when you
      were about to start work? What would you say were
      your main strong points, things you could do well,
      things that you knew would be helpful in this job?
      PROBLE FOR:
      --SKILLS
      --ATTITUDES
      --KNOWLEDGE, CONCEPTS
      GET EXAMPLES, ILLUSTRATIONS
   b. Can you say how you got to know those things,
      develop these skills? Was it courses, jobs,
      workshops, other learning experiences, or what?
   c. When you began as a computer specialist, how were
      you oriented to the job? Was anything done to start
      you off, train you, etc?

3. When you started work with the program -- I'd like to ask you some quesitons about the early phase -- the first few months when you were jsut getting into it.
   a. What kinds of challenges or difficulties did you face? To put it another way, what kinds of skills or knowledge did you realize you needed to function better in the job?
   b. What things do you think you learned during that early time?
   c. And can you say how you learned them? Maybe you could give me an incident or two that would illustrate it. (Might be in a training program, or while you were working.)
   d. (IF NOT CLEAR) And could you tell me how you used that learning in your work in your school? -- an example?
   e. During this whole period, what would you say HELPED your learning the most, and what hindered it?
   f. And can you tell me how you got your support during the early period? Who or what did you go to and how did that help?

4. Now let's come forward in time, later on during your work as you understood your job beter -- how did things go?
   a. First, what would you say were some of the main challenges or difficulties you faced in your work, things you wanted to know how to do better?
   b. And what were some of the things you learned during that period?
   c. And how did you learn them (PROBE for formal, informal courses, supervision, by experience, partnership, etc.)? Can you give me some specific examples or incidents?
   d. (IF NOT CLEAR) And can you tell me how you used that particular learning in your work in your school?
   e. Again, what seemed to help your learning most, and what hindered it?
   f. And what about your support? Where did you go for it? Where did it come from?

5. Finally, have you had any recent learning experiences where you picked up something new that was helpful in your work? Tell me a little about them.

6. We've been focusing mostly on things you've learned that made a difference in the way you worked with people in your school. Stepping back a minute, I'm wondering if there are any things -- personal or professional -- that you've learned that may not show up in direct work in schools, but are nevertheless important. Anything like that?

7. I'd like to reflect back with you over this "learning career" of yours that we've been discussing. Would you say that you have a preferred learning style, a strategy, a way you seem to like to learn things? What does it add up to?

8. Anything else you would like to add?

APPENDIX F

OUTLINE OF INTERVIEW WITH TEACHER

(Start by alluding to introduction from trainer). This is a
visit to get aquainted. It's not an evaluation of you, of
your school program, or of the trainer. I would like to get
a picture of the use of computers in your school. My main
focus is how you have worked with other people along the
way regarding getting help with comptuers. I want to
understand the story of how things have gone from the
beginning until now. I have a number of specific questions
to ask.

1.   Background
      a.   Name
      b.   Job title (or role)
      c.   Thumbnail sketch of your job: what you do, who you
           work with.
      d.   How long have you been teaching?
      e.   How long have you been in this school?

2.   I'm interested in the flavor or feeling in the school.
      a.   Can you give me 3 or 4 adjectives that would
           describe that?
      b.   Can you think back to when your school first got
           involved with comptuers?
           --when was that?
           --why did the school get involved?
           --how did you personally get involved?
      c.   Could you give me a quick sketch of how computers
           are being used right now in your school?
           --how may teachers would you say are really
           involved?
           --what is the role of the principal?
           --what are the main purposes of using computers
             in your school?
           --how is your program set up?
           --do you operate under any guidelines or policies?
           --what does the computer specialist do?

3.   a.   Describe your involvement since the earliest
           implementation of computers here.
      b.   What contact have you had with others who are
           involved? (Especially PROBE for communication,
           cooperation, peer coaching)
      c.   Are there stages or phases that can be identified
           regarding your involvement with the program? Your
           school's involvement?

4. Generally speaking, what do you see as the computer specialist's main role?
    a. What's been <u>her</u> main contribution to your school's program?
    b. Can you give me a few adjectives to describe <u>her</u> <u>style</u>, way of working with people?
    c. What do you see as her special strengths?
    d. Could you tell me about a specific incident when _____ <u>especially helpful</u>?
        --What did <u>she</u> do?
        --Why did you think this was helpful?
        --What skills did you see her using in this situation?
    e. Now let's take another incident.
        --What did <u>she</u> do, in detail?
        --Why did you think this was helpful?
        --What skills did you see her using in this situation?
    f. Do you think her skills and strengths have changed since you've known her? (GET ILLUSTRATIONS AND EXAMPLES)

5. I'm interested in the programs results. For (1) you, (2) other teachers, and (3) the students:
    a. What changes have occurred?
    b. Why do you think these changes happened?
    c. In your opinion, how did _____ contribute to these results?

6. a. What would you say are the necessary ingredients of success in this kind of program?
    b. Specifically, what recommendations do you have for how computer specialists work and who is selected?

7. Do you have anything else to add?

BIBLIOGRAPHY

Ames, C., Gilberstad, N., Sky, N.C., and Strudler, N.
    (1985). <u>Elementary computer program pilot study</u>
    <u>evaluation</u>. Unpublished manuscript, Eugene School
    District 4J, Eugene.

Barbour, A. (1986, February). Computer coordinator
    survey. <u>Electronic Learning</u>, pp. 35-38.

Beaton, C.R. (1985). <u>Identifying change agent strategies,</u>
    <u>skills, and outcomes: The case of district-based staff</u>
    <u>development specialists</u>. Unpublished doctoral
    dissertation, University of Oregon, Eugene.

Berman, P., and McLaughlin, M. (1977). <u>Federal Programs</u>
    <u>supporting educational change, Vol., VIII, Implementing</u>
    <u>and sustaining innovations</u>. Santa Monica, Calif.: Rand
    Corporation.

Fullan, M. (1981). School district and school personnel in
    knowledge utilization. In R. Lehming & M. Kane (Eds.),
    <u>Improving schools: Using what we know</u> (pp.212-252).
    Beverly Hills: Sage.

Gall, M.D., & Renchler, R.S. (1985). <u>Effective staff</u>
    <u>development for teachers</u>: A research based model.
    Eugene, OR: Clearinghouse on Educational Management,
    College of Education, University of Oregon. (ERIC/CEM
    Accession Number EA 017 615).

Huberman, M., & Crandall, D. <u>People, policies, and</u>
    <u>practices: Examining the chain of school improvement,</u>
    <u>Vol. IX</u>. Andover, Mass.: The Network, Inc.; 1982.

Joyce B., and Showers, B. (1983). <u>Power in staff</u>
    <u>development through research on training</u>. Alexandria,
    VA: Association for Supervision and Curriculum
    Development.

Luehrmann, A. (1984, April). The best way to teach
    computer literacy. <u>Electronic Learning, pp. 37-44</u>.

Miles, M.B. (1984, April). <u>The role of the change agent in</u>
    <u>the school improvement process</u>. Abstract of paper
    presented at the annual meeting of the American
    Educational Research Association, New Orleans.

Miles, M.B., Saxl, E.R., and Lieberman, A. (1985). Key skills of educational "change agents": An empirical view. Unpublished manuscript, center for Policy Research and Teachers College, New York, N.Y.

Moursund, D. (1985). The Computer Coordinator. Eugene, OR: International Council for Computers in Education.

Rosenshine, B.V., and Furst, N. (1973). The use of direct observation to study teaching. In R. Travers (Ed.), Second handbook of research on teaching (pp.122-183). Chicago: Rand McNally.